Making the Most of Your
FOOD PROCESSOR

Other cookery titles from Spring Hill, an imprint of How To Books

EVERYDAY COOKING FOR ONE
Wendy Hobson

THE EVERYDAY FISH COOKBOOK
Trish Davies

EVERYDAY THAI COOKING
Siripan Akvanich

THE EVERYDAY HALOGEN FAMILY COOKBOOK
Sarah Flower

MAKE YOUR OWN ORGANIC ICE CREAM
Ben Vear

HOW TO COOK YOUR FAVOURITE TAKEAWAYS AT HOME
The food you like to eat when you want to eat it – at less cost and with more goodness
Carolyn Humphries

Write or phone for a catalogue to:
How To Books
Spring Hill House, Spring Hill Road, Begbroke, Oxford OX5 1RX
Tel. 01865 375794

Or email: info@howtobooks.co.uk

Visit our website www.howtobooks.co.uk to find out more about us and our books.

Like our Facebook page **How To Books & Spring Hill**

Follow us on Twitter **@Howtobooksltd**

Read our books online **www.howto.co.uk**

Making the Most of Your
FOOD PROCESSOR

*How to produce soups, spreads, purees, cakes, pastries
and all kinds of savoury treats*

SUE SIMKINS

SPRING HILL

For David, David and Edie

Published by Spring Hill, an imprint of How To Books Ltd.
Spring Hill House, Spring Hill Road, Begbroke, Oxford OX5 1RX United Kingdom
Tel: (01865) 375794 • Fax: (01865) 379162 • info@howtobooks.co.uk www.howtobooks.co.uk

First published 2013

How To Books greatly reduce the carbon footprint of their books by sourcing their typesetting
and printing in the UK.

British Library Cataloguing in Publication Data
A catalogue record of this book is available from the British Library.

ISBN: 978 1 908974 11 2

Produced for How To Books by Deer Park Productions, Tavistock, Devon
Designed and typeset by Mousemat Design Ltd
Illustrated by Illustrations by Verity Thompson: www.sketchy.org.uk
Printed and bound by in Great Britain by Bell & Bain Ltd, Glasgow

NOTE: The material contained in this book is set out in good faith for general guidance and no
liability can be accepted for loss or expense incurred as a result of relying in particular
circumstances on statements made in the book. Laws and regulations are complex and liable to
change, and readers should check the current position with relevant authorities before making
personal arrangements.

Contents

8   Making Pastry   99

Acknowledgements

Thank you to my family and friends and to everyone who helped (by testing, sampling and general conversation) with the making of this book.

As ever, thank you to Fanny Charles and everyone at the *Blackmore Vale Magazine*.

Thank you, too, to Paul Jackson and Mark Whitley of *The Countryman, Dalesman and Down Your Way*, to Simon McEwan of *Country Smallholding* and to Chris Peachment of *Best of British Magazine* for their continued help and support.

Special thanks to Elodie Martin (aka '*the Queen of Soups*') of Café Elodie in Shaftesbury, Dorset, for sharing her always inspiring ideas so generously; and, once again, to professional baker of many years' standing Frank Dike, for always being there to help with baking queries and ideas.

And, finally, a huge thank you to everyone at How To Books.

Thank you all very much indeed.

Measurements

Both metric and imperial measurements are given for the recipes.
Follow one set of measurements, not a mixture of both, as they are not interchangeable.

OVEN TEMPERATURES										
110°C	120°C	140°C	150°C	160°C	180°C	190°C	200°C	220°C	230°C	240°C
225°F	250°F	275°F	300°F	325°F	350°F	375°F	400°F	425°F	450°F	475°F
Gas ¼	Gas ½	Gas 1	Gas 2	Gas 3	Gas 4	Gas 5	Gas 6	Gas 7	Gas 8	Gas 9

WEIGHT										
25g	50g	75g	100g	150g	175g	200g	225g	250g	300g	450g
1oz	2oz	3oz	4oz	5oz	6oz	7oz	8oz	9oz	10oz	1lb

MEASUREMENTS										
5cm	10cm	13cm	15cm	18cm	20cm	25cm	30cm	35cm	40cm	45cm
2 in	4 in	5 in	6 in	7 in	8 in	10 in	12 in	14 in	16 in	18 in

LIQUID MEASURE										
5ml	15ml	50ml	75ml	100ml	125ml	150ml	200ml	300ml	450ml	600ml
1 tsp	1 tbsp	2 fl oz	3 fl oz	4 fl oz	4½ fl oz	5 fl oz	7 fl oz	½pt	¾pt	1pt

Introduction

Anything that saves you time and money and makes it easier to produce good, wholesome food in your own kitchen is a blessing: and a food processor is a very big blessing indeed for the modern home cook.

With your food processor you can make soups and spreads and purées, slice or grate vegetables, make breadcrumbs and whizz up your own mayonnaise and a variety of sauces and salad dressings.

But, possibly even more enticingly, a simple food processor will give you another level of expertise as a home baker. Light sponge cakes and melt-in-the-mouth pastry and biscuits, which you might have thought too difficult to attempt before, are now within your reach.

What is the best kind of food processor to use?
You don't need to spend a fortune on anything very complicated or fancy; all you need is a simple food processor with the basic chopping blade. A reversible slicer/grater blade may be included as well, which is particularly useful for slicing and grating vegetables for salads. Your food processor may also come with a blender goblet and this is worth having but not essential.

The basic chopping blade is the one you will use most of the time. It's ideal for cake and pastry making, chopping, smoothing and puréeing, beating and folding, cutting and rubbing in.

The reversible slicing and shredding/grating blade – position it one way up for slicing and turn it over for grating – is handy for preparing firmer foodstuffs including fruits and vegetables and hard cheeses.

Please be aware that individual oven performance varies tremendously.

The Well-Stocked Pantry

It's worth keeping a well-stocked store cupboard or pantry. It makes you more organised and it's always good to know you have enough on your shelves to put a meal together if you can't get to the shops.

Include basic baking ingredients and a selection of tinned and dry goods. Keep a few basics in your fridge and freezer as well. As items are used up, make a note on your shopping list to re-stock.

Choose carefully and only include items you know you will use. A vast selection of spices, relishes and fancy oils, for example, that languish on the shelves, unopened, for years are not only a complete waste of money, but will also clutter up your store making it hard to see the items you do want at a glance.

Every few months, give your cupboard or pantry a thorough clean and throw away anything past its sell by date.

Here is a comprehensive list to start you off but you will want to tailor it to suit yourself.

Sweet and Baking
- Almond extract and ground almonds
- Black Treacle
- Golden syrup
- Chocolate, good quality milk and dark: 70% cocoa solids if dark, 34% if milk,
- Cocoa powder
- Coconut, desiccated and creamed in 50g sachets
- Coffee: a jar of good quality instant espresso coffee powder is ideal for baking
- Dried fruit: sultanas, raisins, currants, cranberries, ready to eat apricots, dates
- Flour: plain and wholemeal, only buy self-raising flour if you plan to use it straightaway as it doesn't store well. Adding your own raising agents to plain flour gives a better result – see individual recipes
- Glycerine: excellent for smooth icings
- Honey: runny is a useful all-rounder
- Jam: good staples are strawberry, apricot and raspberry seedless

- Marmalade
- Raising Agents: baking powder, bicarbonate of soda, cream of tartar
- Sugar: caster, granulated, icing sugar, soft light and soft dark brown sugar
- Vanilla extract
- Walnuts: it's worth remembering that walnut halves are often cheaper to buy than broken walnuts

General Basics
- Brandy
- Capers
- Gherkins
- Horseradish sauce
- Marmite
- Mustard: powdered and made English, Dijon and wholegrain are all useful, 'squirty' American mustard is also good
- Oil: have one basic mild oil such as vegetable, sunflower, rapeseed or mild olive and one good extra virgin olive oil
- Olives in brine, black olives are particularly useful
- Passata or good quality tomato sauce for pasta
- Redcurrant jelly
- Relishes: always useful but try to limit yourself to just a few firm favourites
- Tomato ketchup
- Tomato puree
- Vinegar: cider vinegar is excellent for salad dressings; white wine vinegar is also useful. Red wine vinegar, sherry and balsamic are also worth keeping in stock. Include malt vinegar if you eat a lot of fish and chips and a bottle of white spirit vinegar is handy for cleaning jobs around the house.
- Walnuts, pickled: keep a jar of these in stock for adding miraculous flavour to stews and gravies
- Worcestershire sauce

Grains and Pasta
- Cous cous is always useful and quick to prepare
- Pasta shapes: rigatoni or penne, and a shape such as farfalle or fusilli are good standbys, as are spaghetti and egg lasagne sheets, egg noodles are also handy and very quick to prepare
- Pearl barley is useful for soups and stews
- Red split lentils and yellow split peas are useful for soups and dhals
- Rice, long grain, Arborio if you make risotto often

Cans
- Anchovies in oil
- Butterbeans
- Chickpeas
- Kidney beans
- Plum tomatoes
- Salmon: red or pink
- Sardines: in oil and in tomato sauce, try also pilchards
- Tuna, in oil or spring water

Herbs

You can't beat fresh herbs for flavour and it is well worth growing a few yourself: if you are short of space, don't despair, the most commonly used herbs grow well in pots outside the back door

A small bay tree in a pot will keep you well supplied with leaves, otherwise use dried. Parsley (curled or flat leaf, according to preference), chives, rosemary, thyme, sage, oregano or marjoram all grow well in pots. Mint will grow well in a pot for a season but generally needs more space. Basil is notoriously temperamental but will do well in a pot on a sunny window sill for a few months: keep watered and keep picking.

Generally, dried herbs are a poor substitute so exercise caution when buying but a small jar of mixed herbs well within its sell by date is worth having as is dried oregano.

Spices: a very basic 'starter' list
- Black pepper: buy whole and use a pepper mill
- Cayenne pepper
- Cinnamon, ground
- Cumin, ground
- Curry paste
- Chilli powder or chilli paste or puree
- Garlic cloves or puree
- Ginger, ground
- Mixed spice
- Mustard powder
- Sea Salt

Fridge

Remember perishables are a major source of waste, so only buy what you know you will use: any spare vegetables can be whizzed into a 'soup of the week' in your processor. This is also a good way to use up leftover cream.
- Bacon: keep in the fridge only if you use it weekly, otherwise freeze some, see below

- Mature Cheddar is better for cooking than milder varieties
- Butter, salted or slightly salted is better for baking and cooking as there is no need to add extra salt
- Cream: unless you use it constantly, this is best bought as needed
- Eggs: if at all possible keep cool outside the fridge
- Lard or vegetable shortening
- Milk
- Mayonnaise, good quality bottled

Freezer

- Bacon: it's worth having some back bacon in the freezer, if you are very organised, you can freeze the slices separately for fast defrosting
- Bread: If you have room, bread, bagels, crumpets and pitta are always useful
- Chicken livers: useful for pate, risotto or on toast
- Chicken breasts, if you have room a whole chicken can also be useful
- Braising steak
- Milk: if you have room, it's useful to have some semi-skimmed milk in the freezer; smaller bottles will de-frost faster and can be stored in odd corners
- Minced beef, lean
- Sausages
- Smoked salmon
- Vegetables: peas, fine whole green beans, sweetcorn kernels

Freezer Tips

Cheese – grate a block of cheese and store in a tightly sealed freezer bag. Use straight from the freezer for sauces.

Chillies – freeze small ones whole in tightly sealed freezer bags, you can then snip them straight from the freezer into a chilli with kitchen scissors. Quick, easy and they are too cold to burn the skin or irritate!

Croutons – snip leftover crusts of bread into freezer bags and seal tightly. You can fry them as croutons, straight from the freezer.

Onions – when slicing onions, prepare an extra one and freeze in a tightly sealed freezer bag, squash the bag flat for easy defrosting. Fry straight from the freezer for stews and gravies.

Wine – freeze any leftover oddments of wine in tightly sealed freezer bags. Use straight from the freezer to enliven stews and gravies.

Useful Additional Kitchen Equipment

Here are some suggestions for a few tools and bits and pieces that will make cooking with your food processor even easier.

Top priority must go to two or three flexible spatulas (see below) as you will be using them every time you use your food processor. However, they do need specialist care to keep them hygienically clean.

If yours are the kind with a removable head that detaches from the handle, you could be in for a nasty shock if you wash them regularly as one unit. All kinds of nameless filth can collect inside so always wash the handle and scraper parts separately. If you are using a dishwasher, slip the scraper over one of the prongs in the top tray and wash the handle in the cutlery basket. Make sure both parts are dry before putting them together again.

Apple corer
An apple corer is very useful for preparing apples for cooking. The plastic tube-like ones with a plunger are especially handy. Apple corers are much more accurate and safe than the point of a peeler.

Burger press
If you make burgers quite often – *and you will once you have discovered how easy they are to make in your processor* – it is worth buying an inexpensive plastic burger press. They can look a bit flimsy but they are surprisingly robust, last for years, and make good firm burgers.

Ceramic baking beans
Ceramic baking beans conduct the heat more efficiently than dried peas or beans when baking pastry flan cases blind. They help to conduct heat to the inside of the pastry case as well as weighing it down.

Cooling racks
A cooling rack is a must for cooling cakes and biscuits. If you don't have one, you can use a clean grill rack instead.

Flexible rubber or plastic spatulas
These are absolutely essential for scraping the mixture down from the sides of your food processor bowl.

Measuring jug with narrow and accurate non-drip pouring spout
Ideally, you should have a plastic measuring jug with a narrow pouring spout or lip. This is the best way to pour oil slowly down the chute of the processor when making mayonnaise.

Set of measuring spoons
These are essential for accurate measurements, particularly for measuring raising agents for cakes. All dry ingredients should be levelled off.

Lemon reamer
A simple wooden lemon reamer is a quick and easy way to juice a small number of citrus fruits.

Lemon zester
A lemon zester is the best tool for zesting a small amount of citrus fruit.

Large and small palette knives
A small palette knife is invaluable for removing anything baked directly on a baking tray and for loosening cakes and pastries from baking tins. It's also good for spreading icing and buttercream onto cakes. A large palette knife is useful for loosening delicate sponges from the bottom of a loose-bottomed cake tin.

Oven thermometer
It is useful to be able to check the accuracy of your oven dial, especially for cake making. Check the temperature of your oven regularly; electric ovens in particular can deteriorate in performance over time and may need the attention of a professional.

Pastry brush
This is useful for glazing the tops of pastries with water or egg wash.

Plastic picnic knife

If you can get hold of some of those quite strong and robust coloured plastic picnic knives – the kind that come in a set with spoons and forks and have a serrated edge – they are almost as useful as flexible spatulas for scraping mixture and mayonnaise from the bowl of your food processor without scratching.

Rotary food mill

You will find this ideal for fine tuning smooth soups and baby food.

Tea strainer

A tea strainer is useful for sieving small amounts of lemon juice; or, used with a teaspoon as a pusher, it is ideal for ensuring ground mustard is clump free and for dusting icing sugar over cakes.

Icing bag or syringe

A simple icing bag or syringe with a small selection of piping nozzles is useful for topping or filling your cakes with professionally piped icings.

Baking tins

Here are the sizes of baking tins used in this book. Heavier, better-quality baking tins conduct heat more efficiently than anything thin and flimsy and have a longer life.

Large baking tray: A baking tray that just fits comfortably inside your oven is essential for biscuits.
12-cup tart tin: It's useful to have two of these for tarts and little pies.
12-cup muffin tin: As well as muffins, you can use this for fairy cakes. It's useful to have two.
12-cup mini-muffin tins: It's useful to have two of these. They are perfect for tiny versions of the above and for mini jam tarts.

Loose-bottomed cake and sandwich tins

It's useful to have the following sizes:
18cm (7in) cake tin
Pair of 18cm (7in) sandwich tins
20cm (8in) cake tin

Loaf tin

450g (1lb) loaf tin
This is useful for loaf cakes such as lemon drizzle.

Chapter 1

Purées and Baby Food

Your food processor is ideal for making vegetable and fruit purées, which is a great advantage if you have a baby in the house and want to cook ahead; although, for small amounts on a day-to-day basis, you might consider buying a mini-chopper, which is essentially a small food processor.

Please remember, fruit and vegetables for infants should be plain and unseasoned, with no added sugar and absolutely, definitely, no salt whatsoever. Babies need to get used to individual, unadulterated fruit and vegetable flavours; extra sugar is no good for developing teeth, and added salt can have fatal consequences for babies as their tiny developing kidneys are unable to process it.

Keep to a scrupulous hygiene regime
Please remember, everything should be scrupulously clean when you are preparing baby food. All bowls, including the processor bowl and blade, and utensils should be sterilised: you can do this most easily with boiling water from the kettle.

Always consult your health professional when making baby food for the first time.

Puréed Vegetables
Vegetables such as broccoli, Brussels sprouts, carrot, cauliflower, courgette, small tender green beans, parsnip, peas, spinach, swede and turnip can all be lightly cooked in a little water on the hob, or steamed on the hob or in the microwave.

Prepare the vegetables first by cleaning and peeling as appropriate.

Cook Brussels sprouts whole and separate broccoli and cauliflower into medium-sized florets. Tender young beans can be cooked whole. Courgette, carrots, parsnip, swede and turnip can all be cut into shorter lengths or chunks.

Cook until soft and tender but not mushy and purée in the processor with a little of the cooking water.

Cooked peas should be pushed through a sieve or a rotary food mill to remove the skins.

Tip
- Vegetable purées make great vegetable side dishes for older children and adults and are useful for invalids and those getting over an illness. Season to taste with pepper and herbs and the merest touch of salt.

Roast Dinners

Family meals such as chilli and spaghetti bolognese are not suitable for processing for small babies as they contain too much salt and seasoning. Roast dinners, however, minus the gravy and any seasoned sauces, are ideal for processing.

Make sure all the components of meat, mashed or boiled potatoes and vegetables are cooked without salt – you can add salt later for the rest of the family if required. Roast chicken, beef, lamb, pork or turkey, trimmed of fat, skin or gristle, are all suitable but don't give babies gammon, it's too salty.

Cut lean roast meat from the joint into small pieces and put into the processor bowl.

Add unsalted mashed or boiled potatoes and a selection of cooked vegetables such as carrots, peas, broccoli, cauliflower, Brussels sprouts, spring greens or green beans.

Keep to the same proportions of meat and vegetables as you would normally serve to adults and older children, i.e. the amount of vegetables is greater than the amount of meat.

Moisten with a little cooking water from the vegetables and whizz to the required smoothness, depending on the age of your baby. You may have to stop the machine and scrape the purée down from the sides a couple of times with a flexible spatula. Add more cooking water if necessary.

Serve immediately or reheat until piping hot and allow to cool to a suitable temperature before feeding to your baby.

Never, ever, add gravy to your baby's dinner – it contains too much salt, even if you have made it yourself using yeast extract

Puréed Apples and Pears

Puréed cooked apples and pears are both appreciated by young babies and are one of the first weaning foods to be introduced.

- **Apple purée:** Peel, core and slice some dessert apples – cooking apples such as Bramleys are too sour – and cook gently in a little water until tender. Whizz to a purée with a little of the cooking water.

- **Pear purée:** Peel and quarter some ripe pears and remove the tiny central core. Chop each quarter into 4 or 5 pieces and cook gently in a little water until tender. Whizz to a purée with a little of the cooking water.

Tip
- Adults and older children will enjoy pear and apple purées with ice cream or breakfast cereals.

Fresh or Frozen

Serve all these purées fresh, or freeze and use within one month. It's usually safe to freeze fruit and vegetable purées for up to three months in most freezers but it is worth remembering that babies' tastes and requirements change and develop rapidly.

If you are using ice cube trays for freezing baby food, be sure to enclose the trays completely in freezer bags to exclude any air, and secure tightly. This guards against freezer burn and avoids any unpleasant oxidised taste.

Chapter 2

Preparing Meat in the Processor

Food processors aren't really intended for large-scale meat preparation; however, they are handy for small amounts and useful for making the most of leftovers.

Raw Meat

It can be tricky to prepare raw meat in a food processor as raw meat is generally too soft to be cut properly by the chopping blade whizzing round at speed and can quickly turn to mush. The grating and slicing blade is no better either.

What you can do is freeze the meat and process it in short bursts using the normal chopping blade as it starts to defrost – when the meat is still firm yet slightly pliable.

However, the processor works perfectly for home-made hamburgers (see page 42), where you are processing raw meat with breadcrumbs and onions and blending them together.

Cooked Meat

Food processors are good for chopping cold meat finely for a savoury mince or shepherd's pie, but only ever process in short bursts unless you are making meat paste. Use the normal chopping blade.

Nursery Shepherd's Pie

These days we tend to make shepherd's pie with mince but cold roast lamb (or beef) makes an appealing and tasty shepherd's pie with more of a soft 'nursery texture'.

Serves 4 depending on the amount of cold meat left over | Use the normal chopping blade for this recipe.

Approximately 450g (1lb) cold leftover roast lamb or beef

Approximately1kg (2lb) potatoes, plus butter and hot milk for mashing

1 large onion

Oil for frying

1–2 tbsp plain flour

1 tsp black treacle

1 tsp tomato purée

Dash of Worcestershire sauce

150ml (¼pt) hot water

To serve

Crusty bread and butter, boiled or steamed sliced or baby carrots, and peas. There's also something about this style of shepherd's pie that demands a dollop of tomato ketchup.

1. Preheat the oven to 180°C (fan oven) or equivalent.

2. Cut the meat into pieces and whizz very briefly in the food processor: the meat should be fairly coarsely minced, not ground into dust.

3. Fry the onion until golden.

4. Sprinkle the flour over the onion and stir until the flour is absorbed.

5. Stir the black treacle, tomato purée and Worcestershire sauce into the hot water and add gradually to the onions, stirring continuously until smooth.

6. Add the minced meat and bring to the boil.

7. Turn the heat down to moderate and simmer for up to an hour or until the liquid has thickened and reduced. Add more water, or potato cooking water, if it seems dry, but not too much.

8. Meanwhile, boil the potatoes, drain and mash with butter and hot milk, season to taste.

9. When the meat is ready, pour into an oven proof dish (strain off some liquid and retain as gravy if it is too sloppy) and spread the mashed potatoes on top.

10. Make raised lines with a dinner fork across the top and dot with butter so it will brown nicely.

11. Bake in a moderate oven for 20–30 minutes until the top is golden brown.

Minced Chillied Beef

Cold meat left over from a joint of roast beef makes an easy tasty chilli. Use the normal chopping blade for this recipe.

Serves 3-4, depending on the amount of cold leftover meat available

Ideally around 450g (1lb) cold roast beef

1 large onion

1 bell pepper: red, green or yellow

1 stick celery, plus a few green celery leaves, finely sliced

1 finely sliced fresh red chilli or ½ teaspoon chilli powder – or to taste

½ tsp ground cumin

1x 500g jar good quality tomato sauce for pasta

1 x 400g tin of kidney beans in water, drained and refreshed in cold water

Any leftover gravy and/or 1 level tsp Marmite

1 bay leaf

Oil for frying

To serve

Boiled rice or jacket potatoes

1. Cut the meat into pieces and whiz very briefly in the food processor to produce a coarse mince.

2. Fry the onion, pepper and celery until soft. Add the chilli and cumin and cook for a further 2-3 minutes.

3. Add the minced meat, tomato sauce, kidney beans and bay leaf. Add the gravy and or Marmite and bring briefly to the boil.

4. Turn the heat down to moderate and simmer for up to an hour or until the liquid has thickened and reduced. Add a little water if it seems dry.

Cheesy Chilli Shepherd's Pie

You may like to combine elements of the previous two recipes to make an easy and warming supper dish for a winter's evening.

1. Make the Chilli as for the previous recipe and prepare mashed potatoes as for **Nursery Shepherd's Pie.**

2. Spread the mashed potatoes on top. Make raised lines with a dinner fork across the top and scatter with 50g (2oz) of mature Cheddar cheese.

3. Bake in a moderate oven for 20-30 minutes until the top is golden brown.

Chapter 3

Salads, Dressings and Sauces

You can use the reversible slicing/grating blade of your processor to prepare vegetables for nutritious, vibrant salads and the normal chopping blade to make delicious dressings to go with them.

Grating and Slicing Sides of the Reversible Blade

The grater/slicer blade of your food processor will grate and slice vegetables quickly and efficiently with the minimum of fuss.

Food processors produce beautifully fine slices, which is hard for all but the most highly skilled chef to manage with a knife, and grate much more easily than a manual grater, with no fear of grated fingers.

- Push the prepared vegetable down the chute with the motor running and slice or grate half of it.

- Stop the machine and use the pusher to guide the second half through the blade.

Making sauces and dressings
Your food processor will help you make professional sauces and dressings really easily. Instead of taking the lid off the processor bowl every time you add more ingredients, you will be utilising the chute and adding to the mix while the motor is running. Make sure you have a plastic measuring jug or similar, with a narrow pouring spout, on hand to help you pour the oil slowly and accurately.

Winter Vitality Salad

Here's an idea to get you started but you will soon be putting together your own combinations. The idea is to pack as many good things into this as you can. Red cabbage makes a cheerful-looking change from white cabbage and raw parsnip complements the more traditional grated carrot beautifully. Unexpectedly, a slice or two of orange contributes to the overall taste experience; alternatively, mix in some sliced or grated apple. If you have any sesame seeds in the cupboard, a scattering adds extra taste and texture, not to mention antioxidants, vitamins and fibre. All the quantities given are approximate.

Serves 4–6

½ or 1 red cabbage, depending on size

1–2 carrots, peeled

1 parsnip, peeled

Proportionally small amount of onion, peeled

1 or 2 sticks of green celery, de-strung

Apple or slices of orange, sesame seeds (optional)

1. Cut the cabbage into vertical sections that will fit easily into the chute and slice.

2. Grate the carrot and parsnip.

3. Grate or slice the onion.

4. Pile everything into a bowl.

5. Slice the celery and arrange over the top.

6. Finish with orange sliced by hand, sliced or grated apple and a scattering of sesame seeds.

Mustard and Honey Dressing

Use the chopper blade for this recipe.

150ml (¼pt) oil (mild olive, rapeseed, sunflower or vegetable are all suitable)

4 tbsp cider vinegar

2 heaped tsp Dijon mustard

2 generous teaspoons runny honey

1. Put all the ingredients into the processor bowl and whizz until emulsified.

2. Dress the prepared salad or offer separately.

3. Store in a screwtop jar, ideally one with a plastic lid.

Salad suggestions

- **Summer Coleslaw:** Sliced white cabbage, grated carrot and onion, home-made mayonnaise.

- **Radish Salad:** Sliced radish, sliced celery, Mustard and Honey Dressing, snipped chives or snipped fronds of dill or fennel.

  Alternatively, sliced radish, sliced apple and Mustard and Honey Dressing, scattered with cubes of feta or blue cheese, served with or without sliced celery and crumbled walnuts.

- **Baby Beetroot Salad:** Sliced raw baby beetroot, Mustard and Honey Dressing, scattering of snipped chives, served on a bed of mixed baby salad leaves. Slices or segments of orange always work beautifully with beetroot.

- **Courgette Salad:** Sliced raw green and yellow courgette, Mustard and Honey Dressing, scattering of 'soft' fresh herbs such as snipped chives, chervil or young thyme leaves.

- **Grated Carrot Salad:** Grated carrot, Mustard and Honey Dressing, scattering of sesame seeds (optional).

- **Celery and Apple Salad:** Sliced celery and apple, handful of raisins, home-made mayonnaise, scattering of walnuts.

- **Cheese, Celery and Apple Salad:** Sliced celery and apple, cubed mild, firm Cheddar cheese, Mustard and Honey dressing.

- **Wafer Thin Banana:** As well as salad vegetables, you can also try slicing a firm, just-ripe banana with the slicing blade. You end up with a mass of delicate and tantalising wafer-thin slices.

  - Push the banana down the chute with the motor running and slice half of it.

  - Stop the machine and use the pusher to guide the second half through the blade.

Home-made Mayonnaise

Home-made mayonnaise contains uncooked egg and should not be eaten by babies and toddlers, elderly people, pregnant women, people who are already unwell or anyone with a compromised immune system.

Home-made mayonnaise is a real taste of luxury and is something that always seriously impresses guests. It can be tricky to get right by hand but it is simplicity itself in the food processor – provided of course you add the oil very slowly, without rushing, particularly in the early stages. It's also very inexpensive to make as it doesn't use very much of anything. You only need an egg yolk or two, a couple of tablespoons of lemon juice and 150ml (¼pt) of oil to make enough mayonnaise for at least six people.

Lemon juice rather than vinegar
You *can* use vinegar as the acid component of mayonnaise but lemon juice gives excellent results when making mayonnaise at home. Whether it is because it is very slightly less acidic, or whether it is because it is a different type of acid – lemon juice is citric acid whereas vinegar is acetic acid – remains to be seen, but lemon juice works beautifully for home-made mayonnaise, imparting a fresh, mellow flavour, whereas vinegar can taste a little too harsh.

When to use extra-virgin olive oil
You can use any oil you have to hand for a mild-tasting mayonnaise that works with most dishes requiring mayonnaise. Sunflower, rapeseed, vegetable or mild olive oil are all suitable, but occasionally you might want to push the boat out and use extra-virgin olive oil. This gives more of a distinctive, luxurious taste and is essential if you want to make genuine aïoli – see below.

Mayonnaise

All ingredients should be at room temperature.

Makes enough to half-fill an average-size jam jar

2 egg yolks

½ tsp dry mustard powder

2 tsp sieved lemon juice

150ml (¼pt) oil – see above

1½ tbsp warm water

¼ tsp caster sugar

Freshly ground black pepper and a touch of salt to taste

1. Put the egg yolks in the processor bowl with the mustard and one teaspoon of lemon juice.

2. Whizz to mix.

3. Once the egg yolks are fully mixed, keep the motor running and start to add the oil – very, very slowly, virtually one drop at a time – through the chute.

4. As it starts to thicken you can add the oil a little more quickly – but not much – making sure all the oil is completely incorporated before you add the next lot.

5. Continue until all the oil is absorbed.

6. Still with the motor running, add the warm water and the sugar.

7. Add the rest of the lemon juice and test for seasoning: add pepper and salt to taste.

Tips

- Stir the mustard powder through a tea strainer for even distribution without clumping.

- Eggs should be as fresh as possible: fresher eggs emulsify the mayonnaise more efficiently with less chance of splitting.

- As the egg isn't going to be cooked, it's best not to separate it by passing it between the two halves of the shell. Use an egg separator instead, or two dessertspoons. Alternatively, you can try *The Egg Cup Trick*: this involves cracking the egg onto a small plate or saucer, holding an egg cup upside down over the yolk and pouring off the white.

The 'Folded Frill Effect' and Customising Your Own Mayonnaise

Once you start processing the mayonnaise, you will actually be able see the oil and egg yolk emulsifying. As you look down the chute in the lid with the motor running you will see a narrow 'frill' appearing to gather around the edges of the bowl. As you add more oil the 'frill' will become wider and thicker in consistency and then become a double and a treble 'frill', folding over on itself as you add the last few drops.

The ideal flavour and thickness of mayonnaise is very much a matter of personal preference. Once you have made mayonnaise a couple of times and seen how the egg yolk and oil blend together, you may like to tailor the mayonnaise more specifically to your own taste.

Stick with the 150ml (¼pt) oil measurement which, incidentally, also works with one egg yolk, giving an only slightly less rich emulsion.

- Experiment with the amount of warm water, or add no water at all.

- Vary the amount of mustard or try made English or Dijon mustard.

- Try vinegar instead of lemon juice – you may find you like it better, after all. Plain old spirit vinegar is worth trying, or try half lemon juice and half vinegar.

- You may prefer to leave out the sugar.

- Try varying the amount of salt and pepper – or leave the salt out altogether. Try freshly ground white pepper instead of black.

Variations
- **Lemon Mayonnaise:** Stir in some **finely grated lemon zest** to mayonnaise made with lemon juice. Fabulous with fish or chicken.

- **Curried Mayonnaise:** Stir in **a little curry paste or powder** to taste. Lovely with hard-boiled eggs or chicken.

- **Horseradish Mayonnaise:** Stir in **a little horseradish sauce** to taste. Serve with cold roast beef or smoked salmon or trout.

- **Garlic Mayonnaise:** Stir in **finely chopped or crushed garlic** to taste. Wonderful with chips for that Continental experience.

- **Aïoli:** What is the difference between garlic mayonnaise and aïoli? Aïoli *is* garlic-flavoured mayonnaise, but strictly speaking it is mayonnaise made with extra-virgin olive oil enhanced with crushed fresh garlic.

- **Fresh Green Herb Mayonnaise:** Add **1tbsp chopped fresh 'soft' herbs such as dill, chervil, French tarragon, parsley or chives**. You can stir them into the finished mayonnaise or, to incorporate the flavour more fully, add them during processing once half the oil has been absorbed.

You can make a mixed herb mayonnaise or theme the herbs to go with whatever you are serving: tarragon and chervil go well with chicken, for example, parsley with fish and so on.

Try also adding chopped watercress or rocket.

- **Tartare Sauce:** For every **2 rounded tbsp mayonnaise** stir in **1tsp chopped pickled capers**, drained first on kitchen paper, and **1 large or 2 small gherkins, finely chopped** and drained first on kitchen paper. Season with freshly ground black or white pepper. You may like to add **a little chopped fresh parsley** as well.

Storage
- Store all of the above in a sterilised jam jar or similar covered container in the fridge and use within 3 days.

Hollandaise Sauce

Home-made hollandaise sauce contains lightly cooked egg and should not be eaten by babies and toddlers, elderly people, pregnant women, people who are already unwell or anyone with a compromised immune system.

Hollandaise can be tricky, but get yourself off to a good start by utilising your food processor and microwave. The sauce is a simple blend of butter, egg yolks and either vinegar or lemon juice.

110g (4oz) salted or slightly salted butter, diced

3 egg yolks

2 tbsp white wine vinegar or lemon juice

Freshly ground black or white pepper

Salt to taste

To serve

Lightly steamed asparagus or purple-sprouting broccoli. Also use for Eggs Benedict (see page 39)

1. Melt the butter until it is just starting to bubble around the edges. You can do it in the microwave if you like: in a covered bowl on High for about a minute or a little less.

2. Put the egg yolks into the food processor or blender with the vinegar or lemon juice.

3. Whizz for a few seconds.

4. Keep the motor running and pour the melted butter through the chute as slowly as possible. Partially cover the opening with a cloth if you can as it may spit slightly.

5. Once you have added the butter transfer the sauce to a heavy-bottomed saucepan or bowl over a pan of barely simmering water.

6. Heat gently, stirring all the time: a whisk is excellent but you can use a wooden spoon.

7. The moment the sauce thickens slightly remove from the heat and keep whisking or stirring. Don't overheat as hollandaise can split and curdle in the blink of an eye. It will thicken a little more once it is off the heat.

8. Season to taste with pepper: you may also need a touch of salt.

9. Serve immediately.

Note: Unfortunately, hollandaise is not suitable for reheating. To destroy any bacteria that may develop you would need to boil it, which would make the delicate sauce split and separate.

Eggs Benedict

Here is the classic way to serve hollandaise sauce. Perfect for a celebratory breakfast or light supper.

Serves 2

2 muffins

4 fresh eggs

4 slices of ham

Butter and hollandaise sauce to
   finish

1. Split and lightly toast the muffins.

2. Lightly poach the eggs.

3. Lightly butter the muffins and arrange on warmed serving plates.

4. Top with the ham, folded for a professional effect.

5. Sit a poached egg on top and finish with the hollandaise sauce.

6. You may like to grind a very little black pepper over the top.

Tip
- Instead of ham, use slices of smoked salmon.

Chapter 4

Super Savoury Recipes

Food processors make the very best home-made hamburgers in record time: in fact, you may never buy ready-made ones again, especially as you know your own burgers are made from the freshest, most natural ingredients, with absolutely no trace of anything mechanically recovered.

Food processors also make the most wonderful pâtés in a flash: whereas before you may have paid a premium for pâté at smart delicatessen counters, now you can whip some up at home from a tub of chicken livers and a few rashers of streaky bacon.

Proper Home-made Hamburgers

You know exactly what is in a proper home-made hamburger and they are simple and economical to make.

Burgers from ready-minced beef are fine but they don't stay together very well. It's much better to process your meat at home in the food processor with the bread and onion and seasoning. This way everything melds together and the resulting burger is firmer – and much more delicious.

Some keen hamburger lovers may want to use best rump steak but, quite apart from the extravagance, this may not be the best idea: cheaper cuts such as chuck, blade and skirt all have a wonderful flavour and cook particularly well as burgers.

Makes 4–6 burgers

50g (2oz) bread, white or wholemeal

1 small onion, peeled and sliced

250g (8oz) chuck, blade, or skirt steak

½ tsp salt

Freshly ground black or white pepper

Oil for frying

To serve

Sesame seed buns, chunky chips, salad, mayonnaise (see page 35 for home-made mayonnaise), relishes, ketchup, mustard and gherkins

1. Tear the bread into pieces and put into the bowl of your food processor with the onion.

2. Cut the steak into bite-size pieces, season with the salt and pepper and put into the processor.

3. Whizz everything together, stopping the machine from time to time and stirring the mixture round slightly.

4. Once the mixture has started to cling together stop the machine and remove the blade.

5. Shape into burgers (see Tip below).

6. Fry them in a little oil, or grill them if you prefer, keeping the heat moderate in both cases.

7. Allow 10–20 minutes' cooking time.

Tip
- If you don't have one of those handy little plastic burger presses you can easily shape the burgers by hand: it is easier with wet hands, rather than floured. Alternatively, you can get quite good results from pressing them into a round metal biscuit cutter: a small round glass jar, such as a mustard jar, is useful to press the meat down with. Keep the lid on, as it makes it easier to handle.

Variations
- These burgers are very plain but you can season them more specifically if you like. Try adding a good pinch of mustard powder and a few shakes of Worcestershire sauce to the mix, or some Tabasco, finely sliced chilli, or some herbs.

Freezing hamburgers

- The hamburgers freeze beautifully: make sure you freeze them with discs of waxed paper or cellophane between them so that you can separate them easily.

- Store in sealed freezer bags: exclude any air and secure tightly. This guards against freezer burn and avoids any unpleasant oxidised taste. Use within three months.

- You can cook the burgers from frozen; just allow for a few extra minutes' cooking time.

Chicken Liver and Bacon Pâté

With the aid of your food processor, you can whizz up this luxurious, yet economical pâté in a flash, from just a few simple ingredients.

Serves 4–6

380–400g (12–14oz) chicken livers

1 medium onion, finely chopped

4 rashers streaky bacon, cut into small pieces

25g (1oz) butter

1 clove garlic, finely chopped

1 tbsp brandy

A few fresh sage and thyme leaves, finely chopped

Freshly ground black pepper

Salt to taste

To serve

Hot buttered toast or crusty bread, green salad, gherkins or silverskin onions

1. You will need 1 large or 4 small greased ramekins or dishes

2. Inspect the chicken livers and remove any bits of membrane.

3. Snip each liver into 2 or 3 pieces.

4. Fry the onion and bacon in half of the butter until soft.

5. Add the garlic towards the end: this prevents it burning and becoming bitter.

6. Transfer the onion, bacon and garlic to the bowl of your processor while you fry the prepared chicken livers in the remaining butter until just cooked through.

7. Add the livers to the processor with the pan juices.

8. Add the brandy and herbs and whiz until fairly smooth but still with some texture.

9. Season to taste: go easy on the salt.

10. Press into the prepared dishes and cool as quickly as possible before covering with cling film and storing in the fridge.

Chapter 5

Dips and Spreads

In this chapter you'll find delicious nostalgic savoury spreads and great dips. All can be whizzed together in your food processor and are inexpensive to make.

You can whip up a delicious spread from just a bit of cheese and a splash or two of milk and oil. Try it on toasted crumpets, toast, fresh bread and butter or digestive biscuits for a cosy Sunday tea or snack tucked up in front of the fire on a winter's afternoon.

The tempting fish spreads are so quick to make: all are fabulous spread on hot buttered toast with or without an extra squeeze of lemon. Alternatively, use in sandwiches or on buttered rolls.

Spreadable Butter

It's so simple to make your own spreadable butter at home with your food processor. All you need is some softened butter and a little mild oil: sunflower, vegetable and rapeseed all work well.

140g (5oz) softened butter

60ml (2½fl oz) oil (see above)

1. Put the softened butter into your processor bowl and give it a quick whizz.

2. Add 3–4 teaspoons of oil – either remove the lid or pour through the chute – and whizz to incorporate.

3. Scrape the mixture down from the sides with a flexible spatula and add the rest of the oil gradually, whizzing in 3–4 teaspoons at a time.

4. Transfer to a covered container and store in the fridge.

Note: If you feel this is too much oil and not enough butter, reduce the oil to 40–50ml (1½–2fl oz). Experiment until you achieve your preferred combination.

Tip
● The plastic tubs that commercial spreadable butter comes in are ideal for storage.

Lucky Cheese Dip

Simple, savoury and delicious, you can make this with most types of cheese, excluding the very hard or rubbery varieties. Serve with bread or biscuits and vegetable sticks.

110g (4oz) cheese: Cheddar, Double Gloucester, Stilton, Dolcelatte are all ideal

150ml sour cream or crème fraîche

1. Grate or crumble the cheese, as appropriate, and whizz with the sour cream or crème fraîche until smooth.

2. Keep covered in the fridge and use within a couple of days.

Quick and Easy Houmous

It's quick and easy to whip up this delicious houmous in the processor. Sometimes home-made houmous can be a bit too heavy on the tahini: you only need a little for the distinctive houmous taste to come through. In this instance, a domestic teaspoon is easier to use than a proper measuring spoon to measure the tahini.

Mild olive oil, rapeseed, sunflower or vegetable oil are all suitable for houmous.

1 tsp tahini

400g can chickpeas, drained

3 tbsp oil (see above)

Juice of ½ lemon or more to taste

1 garlic clove, peeled and finely chopped or crushed

Salt and freshly ground black pepper to taste

To serve

Warm pitta bread, sticks of raw carrot, celery, bell pepper or cucumber, raw cauliflower florets, quartered tomatoes, olives

1. Stir any oil that has risen to the surface of the jar into the tahini.

2. Whizz the chickpeas with the oil, lemon juice and garlic.

3. Add the tahini and whizz again until smooth.

4. Taste and add more lemon and/or tahini, salt and freshly ground black pepper as required.

5. Store, covered, in the fridge, and eat within 3 days.

Tip
- Try adding a dollop of houmous on the side with roast lamb and roasted vegetables – which should include some roasted red pepper. Serve with warmed pitta bread and olives.

Potted Ham

Try this old-fashioned and economical treat in sandwiches, with crusty bread or rolls, or on hot buttered toast. Add a dab of mustard and a crisp pickle (silverskin onion, gherkin or plain mixed pickles or piccalilli are all good) on the side and serve with some leafy green salad.

Serves 6

1 ham knuckle (ask your local butcher)

1 large onion, peeled and quartered

1-2 carrots, peeled and cut into strips

2-3 sticks of celery, trimmed and cut into strips

1 bay leaf

A few black and/or white peppercorns

To serve

Crusty bread or hot buttered toast, salad leaves and pickles

You will need 6 small 7.5cm (3in) ramekins

You may need to soak your ham knuckle overnight if it's very salty: check with your butcher.

Tip
- Ham knuckle, also known as ham hock, is the same cut as the one used for Thick Pea and Ham Soup (see page 59). It is so delicious and affordable it is also worth cooking for the ham alone, which can be stripped from the bone using a dinner fork to produce succulent, thick shreds of meat, great for chunky sandwiches.

1. Put the ham into a large saucepan with the onion, carrot, celery, bay leaf and peppercorns. Pour over enough water to cover.

2. Bring to the boil, skim off any froth and simmer fairly briskly for 2 to 3 hours, or until the ham is virtually falling off the bone. Check from time to time, adding more water if necessary.

3. Once cooked, take the ham from the stock, cover with foil and leave to rest in a warm place for 20 minutes or so. Reserve the stock and keep in a cool place.

4. Once the ham has rested, use a dinner fork to take all the ham off the bone. Remove and discard as much fat as you can, but don't worry about the odd tiny bit here and there as it will add to the flavour and texture. You should have about 225g (8oz) of meat or thereabouts.

5. Put the meat into the processor bowl with a couple of tablespoons of the stock. Whizz and then add a couple more tablespoons of stock.

6. Repeat until you have added about 10 tablespoons in all and the ham is the texture of smooth pâté and is slightly clumping together. Add a spot more stock if it seems too dry. You shouldn't need any further seasoning at all as the flavour is already delicious.

7. Divide the mixture between 6 small 7.5cm (3in) ramekins. Alternatively, you can use one large dish or container.

8. Once the ham is all potted, take a teaspoon of the cooking liquid at a time and pour over the surface of each ramekin of ham to add extra moisture: adjust quantities accordingly if you are using larger containers.

9. Cover with foil or cling film. Store in the fridge and use within 48 hours.

Note on hygiene: Make sure your hands are scrupulously clean as you remove the meat from the bone: if you can, it's better to use a dinner fork and a short-handled sharp knife.

Potted Beef

Here's another old-fashioned favourite, to spread on hot buttered toast or crusty bread, or use to fill lunchtime sandwiches.

Chuck steak, blade or skirt are all economical cuts, which respond well to long, slow cooking and are full of flavour. Don't try to remove any slight bits of membrane or connective tissue before cooking: this all helps with the flavour.

Leave the meat in its original pieces and, similarly, don't cut the vegetables smaller than suggested, otherwise you will have too many inconveniently sized pieces to remove from the stock at the end.

Serves 6

225g (8oz) chuck steak, blade or skirt (ask your local butcher)

Oil for frying,

1 large onion, peeled and quartered

1-2 carrots, peeled and cut in half lengthwise

2-3 sticks of celery, trimmed and cut in half lengthwise

1 bay leaf

1-2 tbsp Worcestershire sauce

1 tbsp soft dark brown sugar

Approximately 1.5 litres (2½ pt) hot water

Salt to taste

To serve

Crusty bread or hot buttered toast, salad leaves and pickles

You will need 6 small 7.5cm (3in) ramekins

Tip

- Refrigerate or freeze any leftover stock from the beef and use for adding to soups or curries. Use any refrigerated stock within 48 hours.

1. Brown the beef in the oil.

2. Put the prepared vegetables into a clean pan with the water, bay leaf, Worcestershire sauce and brown sugar. Stir and add the browned beef – including all the beefy residue from the pan.

3. Bring everything to the boil and simmer gently, partially covered with a lid, for 2–3 hours until the beef is falling apart and very tender. Check from time to time, adding more water if necessary.

4. Once cooked, remove the beef from the stock and transfer to a warm plate. Cover with foil and leave to rest in a warm place for 20 minutes or so.

5. Strain and reserve the stock and keep cool.

6. Put the meat into the processor bowl with 2 tablespoons of the stock. Season lightly with salt.

7. Whizz and then add a couple more tablespoons of stock. Repeat until you have added about 10 tablespoons in all and the beef is a fairly smooth, pale paste and is slightly clumping together. Add a spot more stock if it seems too dry. Check for seasoning.

8. Divide the mixture between 6 small 7.5cm (3in) ramekins. Alternatively, you can use one large dish or container.

9. Once the beef is all potted, take a teaspoon of the cooking liquid at a time and pour it over the surface of each ramekin of beef to add extra moisture: adjust quantities accordingly if you are using larger containers.

10. Once cold, cover with foil or cling film. Store in the fridge and use within 48 hours.

Original Cheddar Spread

You don't need any extra seasoning: the flavour of the cheese speaks for itself. Sunflower, rapeseed, vegetable or mild olive oil are all suitable for this spread.

Makes enough to fill, or almost fill, a large 8.5cm (3½in) ramekin

110g (4oz) Cheddar cheese

1 tbsp semi-skimmed milk

3–4 tsp oil (see above)

1. Grate the cheese using the grating side of the grating/slicing blade.

2. Remove the blade and cheese and fit the chopping/mixing blade.

3. Return the cheese to the processor bowl, add the milk and whizz briefly.

4. Add a teaspoon of oil and whizz again.

5. Add the rest of the oil and whizz until smooth.

Red Hot Cheese Spread with Chilli

The chilli complements the cheese and gives an exciting bite.

Makes enough to fill, or almost fill, a large 8.5cm (3½in) ramekin

Small piece of fresh red chilli (or pinch of chilli powder to taste)

110g (4oz) Cheddar cheese

1 tbsp semi-skimmed milk

3–4 tsp sunflower oil (see above)

1. Snip the chilli into small pieces with sharp kitchen scissors.

2. Grate the cheese using the grating side of the grating/slicing blade.

3. Remove the blade and cheese and fit the chopping/mixing blade.

4. Return the cheese to the processor bowl; add the milk and whizz briefly.

5. Add a teaspoon of oil and whizz again.

6. Add the rest of the oil and the snipped chilli (or chilli powder) and whizz until smooth.

Sardine and Tomato Spread

This recipe is very economical; it makes more than enough spread for two, whereas a tin of sardines seems barely enough for one. This and each of the following fish recipes will make sufficient to fill, or almost fill, a ramekin measuring 8.5cm (3½in) in diameter.

1 x 120g tin sardines in tomato sauce

2 tsp mild oil

Freshly ground black or white pepper to taste

Squeeze of lemon juice to taste

1. Empty the sardines and tomato sauce into the processor bowl.

2. Add the oil, pepper and lemon juice.

3. Whizz until smooth, stopping a couple of times to scrape the paste down from the sides of the bowl with a flexible spatula.

4. Check for seasoning.

5. Refrigerate and use within 24 hours.

Tuna Spread

1 x 185g tin of tuna in spring water, drained

2 tsp mild, flavourless oil

2 tsp lemon juice – or to taste

Freshly ground black or white pepper

1. Empty the tuna into the food processor bowl.

2. Add the oil, lemon juice and pepper.

3. Whizz until smooth, stopping a couple of times to scrape the paste down from the sides of the bowl with a flexible spatula.

4. Check for seasoning. You may need a touch of salt.

5. Refrigerate and use within 24 hours.

Tuna and Mayonnaise Spread

1 x 185g tin of tuna in spring
  water, drained

2 tsp mayonnaise

2 tsp lemon juice – or to taste

Freshly ground black or white
  pepper

1. Empty the tuna into the food processor bowl.

2. Add the mayonnaise, lemon juice and pepper.

3. Whizz until smooth, stopping a couple of times to scrape the paste down from the sides of the bowl with a flexible spatula.

4. Check for seasoning.

5. Refrigerate and use within 24 hours.

Salmon Spread

You can use either pink or red salmon for this recipe.

1 x 212g tin of salmon, drained

2 tsp mild, flavourless oil

2 tsp lemon juice – or to taste

Freshly ground black or white
  pepper

1. Empty the salmon into the food processor bowl.

2. Add the oil, lemon juice and pepper.

3. Whizz until smooth, stopping a couple of times to scrape the paste down from the sides of the bowl with a flexible spatula.

4. Check for seasoning.

5. Refrigerate and use within 24 hours.

Salmon and Mayonnaise Spread

1 x 212g tin of salmon, drained

2 tsp mayonnaise

2 tsp lemon juice, or to taste

Freshly ground black or white pepper

1. Empty the salmon into the bowl of your food processor.

2. Add the mayonnaise, lemon juice and pepper.

3. Whizz until smooth, stopping a couple of times to scrape the paste down from the sides of the bowl with a flexible spatula.

4. Check for seasoning.

5. Refrigerate and use within 24 hours.

Anchovy Paste

This is similar to Gentleman's Relish or Patum Peperium: perfect on triangles or wide soldiers of buttered toast. Spread thinly as a little goes a long way.

2 x 50g tins of anchovies in oil

Squeeze of lemon juice

Pinch of cayenne pepper

Freshly ground black pepper

1. Whizz the anchovies, including their oil, and the lemon juice, cayenne and black pepper together in the processor.

2. Once you have a smooth paste, transfer it to a small dish or ramekin, cover and store in the fridge.

3. Serve spread thinly on triangles or wide soldiers of hot buttered toast.

4. Store, covered, in the fridge for up to a week.

Tip
- Add leftover paste sparingly to casseroles and gravies for an extra savoury flavour in place of salt.

Chapter 6

Soups

Food processors are fantastic for home-made soups. Not only does the processor give a smooth texture but the processing seems to extract extra flavour from the ingredients. Where you have fried some of the vegetables beforehand, such as onions, the processor enables the small amount of oil from the frying to be evenly distributed throughout the soup giving a more luscious texture or 'mouth-feel'.

Once you become proficient at soup-making you will want to make up your own soups from ingredients you have to hand. With the help of your food processor, you can create delicious and nourishing soups from what's in season and on offer in the shops or vegetable plot, left in your fridge, or even from the remains of Sunday's roast. Here are some tips and recipes to get you started.

General Pointers for Soup Making

- The majority of soups benefit from a base of fried onions, plus additional leeks and celery if available: this adds depth of flavour and mellowness.

- Some finely chopped garlic, added to the onions towards the end of their cooking time, gives even more flavour – but be careful not to overcook the garlic or it can become burnt and bitter.

- If you are using spices or sliced fresh chillies, temper them first by frying in a little oil for a few minutes to soften any harshness and develop the flavour.

- When cooking vegetables in water add some peeled and sliced aromatic vegetables to create an integral stock: a quartered onion, a couple of carrots quartered lengthwise, a couple of sticks of celery (see below) are all good at adding depth of flavour.

- Celery is the most fantastic soup flavour maker and comes with its own 'free herb' attached: celery leaves are a herb in their own right so don't throw them away. The main bright green leaves from green celery are fresh and tangy; the small yellow leaves tucked in the very centre of the sticks and the yellow leaves from white celery are mellower. Both are well worth chopping and adding to soups towards the end of cooking. The celery sticks are dual-purpose: slice them and fry with onions for the base, and add a couple of sticks to vegetable cooking water as stock vegetables to impart extra flavour.

- Leeks are another great soup vegetable: they add depth of flavour and give the soup a lovely silky texture.

- A few sprigs of parsley, flat-leaf or curly, are also useful: include the stalks as much of the flavour comes from the stalks. Other good flavour performers are parsnips, peeled chunks of celeriac and sprigs of lovage. You can fish out the stock vegetables with a slotted spoon once they have done their job if you don't want them in the finished soup.

- Avoid making your soup too thin at the outset by straining off some of the cooking water before processing the vegetables. Reserve the strained liquid to adjust the thickness later.

- Refrigerate any leftover stock and use for gravies and casseroles over the next couple of days.

Green Pea Soup

Topped with bacon and croutons this glorious soup makes a delicious and nourishing winter meal. Sieving the peas before blending with the rest of the soup removes all the skins and gives the soup a beautifully smooth texture.

Serves 4

450g (1lb) frozen peas

Approximately 450g (1lb) potatoes suitable for mashing

2 or 3 carrots

2 or 3 sticks of celery, including leaves

A few sprigs of parsley, including stalks, if available

1 large onion

1 or 2 leeks, if available

Oil for frying

A little salt and freshly ground black or white pepper

To serve

Fried diced bacon, croutons, freshly ground black pepper

1. Cook the peas in water in the normal way for 8–10 minutes. Peel and prepare the potatoes as you would normally for mashed potatoes. Peel the carrots and clean the celery.

2. Add the carrots, celery and parsley to the potatoes and cook all together for 20–25 minutes or until tender.

3. Put the peas in the food processor with a little of their cooking water (discard the rest) and whizz to a purée. Push through a sieve or a rotary food mill and set aside.

4. Peel and slice the onion and peel, clean and slice the leek. Cook gently in the oil until soft but not coloured. You can put a lid on the pan if you like, so they half fry, half steam.

5. Strain the cooked potatoes and other vegetables and reserve the cooking water. Remove the celery and parsley and discard.

6. Mash the potatoes and carrot together and put into the food processor with the onion and leek. Whizz together until smooth.

7. Put into a large clean pan with the sieved peas and stir together. Stir in some of the cooking water until you have the thickness you like. Season to taste with salt and a few twists of pepper, and heat through.

8. To serve, fry some diced bacon in a little oil and in another pan fry a couple of slices of bread cut into small squares in a little oil. Serve the soup in deep bowls with the bacon and croutons and freshly ground pepper.

Variations
- **Garlic Croutons:** Spread the bread very lightly with garlic butter before cutting and frying.

- **Marmite Croutons:** Spread the *lightest* smear of Marmite over both sides of each slice before cutting and frying.

Leek and Potato Soup

Leeks give soup a lovely silky consistency and are always worth adding to any vegetable soup. It's no trouble to add a few traditional stock vegetables to the cooking water and make a natural-tasting integral stock. As with mashed potatoes, hot milk gives a better consistency than cold, so warm your milk before adding to the soup.

Serves 4

2 large onions

Approximately 350g (½lb) leeks

Approximately 700g (1¾lb)
  potatoes suitable for mashing

2 carrots

3–4 sticks of celery

A few sprigs of parsley, including
  stalks, if available

Freshly ground white pepper

Salt to taste

100ml (4fl oz) semi-skimmed milk,
  warmed

Oil for frying

To serve

Crusty bread, snipped chives or
  fried sliced spring onions

Tip
- Try adding a dash of dry (but not extra dry) vermouth to the soup at the final heating through for an intriguing herbal flavour, but go easy as too much can be overpowering. For a special occasion you might also like to add a dash of cream just before serving.

1. Peel and slice one of the onions.

2. Peel and slice the leeks, discarding the tough green parts.

3. Fry the onion and leeks gently in the butter or oil until soft and translucent but not coloured. You can put a lid on the pan if you like, so they half fry, half steam.

4. Peel the potatoes and cut into chunks.

5. Peel the carrots and cut lengthways and then in half.

6. Clean and trim the celery and cut in the same way.

7. Peel and quarter the second onion.

8. Add the carrot, celery, onion and parsley to the potatoes and boil in unsalted water until tender.

9. Drain the potatoes, reserving the cooking water, and remove and discard the carrot, celery, onion and parsley.

10. Roughly mash the potatoes with a fork and put them into the bowl of your food processor with the softened onions and leeks.

11. Add about 5 tablespoons of the cooking water, some pepper and salt and whizz.

12. Scrape the mixture down from the sides and add another 4 or 5 tablespoons of cooking water.

13. Repeat and then add the warm milk.

14. Check for seasoning – you may need more salt – and put into a clean pan and heat through.

15. Add more cooking water for a thinner consistency.

16. Serve with crusty bread. A few chives snipped over the top work well, or slice some spring onions diagonally and fry lightly in butter or oil as an alternative topping.

Thick Pea and Ham Soup

This is a really old-fashioned pea soup, the kind made with dried peas that you soak overnight. You can get your ham knuckle from your local butcher at a very reasonable price. The soup won't be bright green like a soup made with fresh or frozen peas but a kind of murky yellow.

Serves 4–6

1 ham knuckle

450g (1lb) dried split peas

1 large onion

Oil for frying

Water to cover

1-2 carrots, peeled and cut into strips

2-3 sticks of celery, trimmed and cut into strips

1 bay leaf

Freshly ground white or black pepper (optional)

To serve

Crusty bread or sandwiches made from the ham knuckle

Tip
- To dry the soaked peas, try using two colanders: drain them in one, put a clean tea towel in the other, transfer the peas and fold the cloth over. If you put the peas into the hot oil when they are wet, they will spit all over your hands and wrists in a very painful way!

1. You may need to soak your ham knuckle overnight if it's very salty: check with your butcher.

2. Soak the peas in cold water overnight.

3. When you are ready to make the soup, drain the soaked peas and try to get them as dry as possible (see Tip below).

4. Peel and slice the onion and fry in the oil until soft and just starting to colour.

5. Put the peas into the pan and turn and coat with the oil.

6. Put the ham into a large saucepan with the onion and peas, carrot, celery and bay leaf.

7. Pour enough water over to cover: approximately 3 litres (6 pt) or so.

8. Bring to the boil, skim off any froth and simmer fairly briskly for 2 to 3 hours, stirring from time to time, or until the peas are soft and the ham is falling off the bone. Add more water if necessary.

9. Take out the ham and the bay leaf, drain off some of the liquid and reserve.

10. Whizz all the rest in the food processor in two batches.

11. Have a clean pan standing by. If the soup seems a bit thick add some of the reserved cooking liquid.

12. Using a dinner fork, take all the ham off the bone. Either add some to the soup or reserve it for sandwiches.

13. Check for seasoning. You are unlikely to need salt and you may not even need pepper either as the soup is so flavoursome as it is.

14. Make sure it is all heated through: it will spit so a spatter guard is useful.

15. Serve with plenty of crusty bread or sandwiches made from the ham and a touch of mustard.

Baked Pumpkin Soup

Baking the pumpkin beforehand gives the soup a beautifully concentrated flavour. Once baked, it's also easier to cut into to remove the seeds and scoop out the flesh.

Serves 4

1 medium pumpkin, approximately 1.5kg (3½lb) uncooked weight

2 large onions

2–3 sticks celery including leaf

Oil for frying

Approximately 1 level dssp medium curry paste

Approximately 675g (1½lb) potatoes

To serve

Crusty bread or croutons

1. Preheat the oven to180°C (fan oven) or equivalent.

2. Wipe any splashes of mud from the pumpkin with a damp cloth and lightly grease the bottom. Put it into a fairly shallow baking dish and make some small slits in the top.

3. Bake for about an hour or until the skin is soft. Test with the point of a kitchen knife: if it's cooked there will be no resistance. Leave until cool enough to handle.

4. Meanwhile, peel and thinly slice one of the onions and 1 stick of celery.

5. Fry the onion and celery gently in the oil until soft and translucent but not coloured.

6. Stir in the curry paste.

7. Peel the potatoes and cut into chunks. Clean and trim the rest of the celery, cut lengthways and then in half.

8. Peel and quarter the second onion.

9. Add the celery and onion to the potatoes and boil in unsalted water until tender.

10. Drain the potatoes, reserving the cooking water, and remove and discard the celery and onion.

11. Roughly mash the potatoes and put them into the bowl of your food processor with the onions and leeks.

12. Scoop the flesh from the pumpkin skin and add to the potato mixture.

13. Add about 5 tablespoons of the potato cooking water, some pepper and salt and whizz. Scrape the mixture down from the sides and add another 4 or 5 tablespoons of cooking water.

14. Warm through in a clean pan, adding more water for a thinner consistency if necessary.

15. Serve with crusty bread or croutons.

Tip
- The grey-green winter squash variety 'Crown Prince' is superior to the large traditional orange pumpkins for soup-making: the flesh is denser and more flavourful, whereas traditional varieties can be insipid and watery.

Lentil Soup

This is another 'winter warmer'-type soup, but the curry flavour makes it equally welcome on a wet and chilly summer's day.

Serves 4

225g (8oz) red split lentils

1 large onion

Oil for frying

1 stick of celery, sliced

1 level dssp curry paste, such as Madras

2-3 carrots, peeled and cut fairly small

2-3 additional sticks of celery, trimmed and cut fairly small

845ml (1½pt) water

1 bay leaf

To serve

Warm naan bread or chapatti, crisply fried onions

1. Wash the lentils in cold water and drain. Try to get them as dry as possible.

2. Peel and slice the onion and fry in the oil with the sliced celery stick, until soft and just beginning to colour.

3. Stir in the curry paste.

4. Add the carrots and celery and the drained lentils.

5. Turn and stir everything in the hot oil until coated.

6. Add the water and bay leaf.

7. Bring to the boil then turn down and simmer fairly briskly for about 1 hour or until the lentils are soft and most of the water has been absorbed.

8. Stir from time to time and add more water if necessary. It will spit so cover with a spatter guard or rest the lid loosely across the top.

9. Once the soup has cooked, remove the bay leaf and whizz it in the processor until smooth.

10. Check for seasoning. If you are not serving it immediately, transfer to a clean pan and keep warm on a low heat.

11. Serve with warm naan bread or chapatti. A garnish of onions, fried until they are quite dry and crispy, works well.

Beef Mulligatawny Soup

Tasty and warming, this well-known hot and spicy soup is very comforting on a cold night. It can also be made with chicken or lamb.

Serves 4

225g (8oz) chuck steak, blade or skirt (ask your local butcher)

A little oil for frying

1 large onion, cut into 4

1 level dssp curry paste, such as Madras, or curry powder, according to personal taste

1-2 carrots, peeled and cut in half lengthwise

2-3 sticks of celery, trimmed and cut in half lengthwise

Approximately 1.5 litres (2½pt) hot water

Handful of sultanas

To serve

50-110g (2-4oz) long-grain rice, natural yoghurt (optional)

1. Brown the beef in the oil.

2. In another pan, fry the onions until they are soft and starting to turn golden. Add the curry paste or powder and stir in. Cook gently for a few moments to allow the flavour to develop.

3. Add the prepared vegetables and hot water to the onions. Stir and add the browned beef, scraping off and including all the beefy residue from the pan.

4. Bring everything to the boil and then simmer gently, partially covered with a lid, for 2–3 hours until the beef is falling apart and very tender. Check from time to time, adding more water if necessary.

5. Once cooked, remove the beef from the pan and transfer to a warm plate. Cover with foil and allow to rest for a few moments.

6. Meanwhile, remove the celery from the stock and discard. Cut the carrots into smaller pieces and return.

7. Put the meat into the processor bowl and add a couple of tablespoons of the stock.

8. Whizz and then add a couple more tablespoons of stock.

9. Whizz again and then add more stock and the vegetables.

10. Add more stock until the soup is the consistency you want. You may need to do this in two batches.

11. Put your rice on to cook and transfer the soup to a clean pan. Add the sultanas to the soup and heat it through gently while the rice is cooking.

12. Serve the soup in warmed bowls with a spoonful or two of rice in the bottom. You can also dollop some natural yoghurt on top.

Parsnip and Coconut Soup with Chilli, Ginger and Garlic

Ready to eat within half an hour

This velvety, soothing soup is quick and simple to make. It's extremely economical, packed full of goodness and makes a nourishing lunch or supper served with crusty bread.

Serves 4

Approximately 1kg (2lb) parsnips

Approximately 1 litre (2pt) cold water

Approximately 3 celery sticks including green leaf

1 x 50g (2oz) sachet creamed coconut

1 clove garlic

½ teaspoon powdered ginger or small piece of ginger root, grated

½ fresh red chilli, finely chopped, or ½ teaspoon chilli powder, or to taste

Oil for frying

Salt to taste

To serve

Crusty bread, sliced chilli

1. Peel the parsnips, cut them into even-sized pieces and put into a pan with enough cold water to cover.

2. Cut the celery sticks in half and add to the pan.

3. Grate the coconut and add to the pan.

4. Fry the garlic, ginger and chilli in a little oil for about 3 minutes and add to the pan.

5. Bring to the boil and turn down the heat and simmer for around 15 minutes until the parsnip is tender.

6. Remove the celery and discard.

7. Drain off some of the cooking liquid and reserve.

8. Whizz the soup until smooth, adding small amounts at a time of the reserved liquid until you have the consistency you prefer. Check for seasoning, you may need to add a little salt.

9. Garnish with some thinly sliced chilli and serve with crusty bread.

Sweet Potato and Coconut Soup

Ready to eat within half an hour

Here is a similar soup to the previous one made with sweet potato: smooth and full of flavour.

Serves 4

Approximately 1kg (2lb) sweet potato

Approximately 1 litre (2pt) cold water

Approximately 3 celery sticks including green leaf

1 x 50g sachet creamed coconut

1 clove garlic

½ tsp powdered ground coriander, or to taste

½ tsp ground cumin, or to taste

Oil for frying

To serve

Crusty bread

1. Peel the sweet potatoes and cut into even-sized pieces. Put into a pan with enough cold water to cover.

2. Cut the celery sticks in half and add to the pan.

3. Grate the coconut and add to the pan.

4. Fry the garlic, coriander and cumin in a little oil for about 3 minutes and add to the pan.

5. Bring to the boil and turn down the heat and simmer for around 15 minutes until the sweet potato is tender.

6. Remove the celery and discard.

7. Drain off some of the cooking liquid and reserve.

8. Whizz the soup until smooth, adding small amounts at a time of the reserved liquid until you have the consistency you prefer.

9. Serve with crusty bread. You can also sprinkle a little desiccated coconut on top.

Curried Parsnip and Apple Soup

If you are short of parsnips, or would like a milder flavour, use half parsnip, half potato.

Serves 4

2 large onions

Oil for frying

Approximately 1 level dssp medium curry paste (or to personal taste)

Approximately 1kg (2lb) parsnips

Approximately 1 litre (2pt) cold water

Approximately 3 celery sticks including green leaf

1–2 cooking apples or tart green eating apples

To serve

Crusty bread, thinly sliced fried celery, fried buttered sultanas

1. Peel and slice the onions and fry in the oil until soft and golden.

2. Add the curry paste and stir in. Cook gently for a few moments to allow the flavour to develop. Set aside.

3. Peel the parsnips, cut them into even-sized pieces and put into a pan with enough cold water to cover.

4. Cut the celery sticks in half and add to the pan.

5. Bring to the boil and turn down the heat and simmer for around 15 minutes until the parsnip is tender.

6. Meanwhile, peel, core and slice the apple and add to the pan for the last 5 minutes of cooking.

7. Remove the celery and discard.

8. Drain off some of the cooking liquid and reserve.

9. Add the curried fried onions and whizz the soup until smooth, adding some of the reserved liquid until you have the consistency you prefer.

10. Serve with crusty bread and garnish with thinly sliced celery or sultanas fried in butter or oil.

Courgette and Blue Cheese Soup

Ready to eat within half an hour

Fans of blue cheese will love this tasty, tangy soup. Quick and easy to make, and ready within half an hour, the only additional seasoning you need is a bit of pepper.

Serves 4

1 large onion

Oil for frying

5-6 fresh young medium courgettes

Water to cover

Approximately 110g (4oz) blue cheese, chopped, crumbled or grated

Freshly ground black or white pepper

To serve

Crusty bread

1. Peel and slice the onion and fry in the oil in a deep saucepan until soft and golden.

2. Chop the courgettes – there is no need to peel – and put in the pan with water to cover.

3. Simmer for approximately 10–15 minutes until just tender.

4. Drain off some of the cooking liquid and reserve.

5. Add the blue cheese to the pan and cook briefly until just melted.

6. Whizz the soup until smooth, adding some of the reserved liquid if necessary until you have the consistency you prefer. Season with freshly ground black or white pepper.

7. Serve with crusty bread.

Tip
- If seeds have begun to form in the courgettes, cut them lengthways and use a teaspoon to scrape out the seedy bits.

Courgette and Brie Soup

Ready to eat within half an hour

You can make a tasty soup with tender young courgettes and brie. Follow the previous recipe, making sure the courgettes aren't too large, and substitute brie for the blue cheese.

Cauliflower and Cheese Soup

Here's a soup version of the much-loved cauliflower cheese.

Serves 4

1 large onion

Oil for frying

A couple of medium potatoes

Approximately 1 litre (2pt) cold
water

1 cauliflower head approximately,
400–500g (14oz–1lb) in weight,
cut into florets

Approximately 110g (4oz) Cheddar
cheese, grated

Freshly ground black or white
pepper

To seve

Crusty bread

1. Peel and slice the onion and fry in the oil until soft and golden.

2. Peel and slice the potatoes and put in a pan with the water.

3. Bring to the boil and simmer for approximately 20–25 minutes until tender.

4. Either add the cauliflower to the potatoes for the final 4–5 minutes of cooking until tender or steam the cauliflower for 4–5 minutes until tender.

5. Drain off some of the cooking liquid and reserve.

6. Whizz the soup until smooth, adding some of the reserved liquid if necessary until you have the consistency you prefer.

7. Transfer to a pan and heat through – don't boil as this will impair the flavour.

8. Add the grated cheese to the pan and cook briefly until just melted.

9. Check for seasoning: you may need a little pepper.

10. Serve with crusty bread. A little fried bacon scattered over the top is a nice addition.

Tip
- Be sure not to overcook the cauliflower: as with all brassicas, once overcooked – even by a minute – the sulphurous compounds, released as the cell walls collapse, come to the fore. If you have a steamer, steaming is a more effective method of cooking cauliflower and broccoli than boiling.

Blue Cheese and Broccoli Soup

Here's another cheese-themed soup, tasty and full of goodness.

Serves 4

1 large onion

Oil for frying

A couple of medium potatoes

Approximately 1 litre (2 pt) cold
  water

1-2 heads of broccoli weighing
  approximately 400-500g
  (14oz-1lb), cut into florets

Approximately 110g (4oz) blue
  cheese

Freshly ground black or white
  pepper

To serve

Crusty bread

1. Peel and slice the onion and fry in the oil until soft and golden.

2. Peel and slice the potatoes and put in a pan with the water.

3. Bring to the boil and simmer for approximately 20–25 minutes until tender.

4. Either add the broccoli to the potatoes for the final 4–5 minutes of cooking until tender or steam the broccoli for 4–5 minutes until tender.

5. Drain off some of the cooking liquid and reserve.

6. Whizz the soup until smooth, adding some of the reserved liquid if necessary until you have the consistency you prefer.

7. Transfer to a pan and heat through – don't boil as this will impair the flavour.

8. Add the blue cheese to the pan and cook briefly until just melted.

9. Check for seasoning: you may need a little pepper.

10. Serve with crusty bread.

Tip
- Be sure not to overcook the broccoli: as with all brassicas, once broccoli is overcooked – even by a minute – the lovely sweet nutty taste is lost and the sulphurous compounds, released as the cell walls collapse, come to the fore. If you have a steamer, steaming is a more effective method of cooking broccoli than boiling.

Nettle Soup

Try this nourishing soup in spring: the best time to pick suitable young nettle tops is throughout April and May. You will need to wear rubber gloves to pick and handle the nettles before they are cooked. It's generally agreed that simmering nettles for 5 minutes removes all the stinging elements.

Young nettle tops are an excellent source of calcium, magnesium, iron and numerous trace elements plus a range of valuable vitamins.

Serves 4

2 large onions

1 further onion

Knob of butter or a couple of tbsp oil for frying

1-2 carrots

4 medium-sized potatoes

1-2 sticks celery including green leafy tops

1 average-sized colander of young nettle tops (harvested well away from busy roads and traffic pollution)

Salt and freshly ground black pepper

To serve

Crusty bread, croutons, fried diced bacon

Tip
● Nettles don't always have to take centre stage as the main soup component: a couple of handfuls are quickly gathered in springtime and are enough to add extra nutrition and subtle flavour to most green vegetable soups. Nettles and leeks are a particularly tasty combination; try adding some to **Leek and Potato Soup** (page 58).

1. Peel and slice the 2 large onions and fry gently until soft and golden.

2. Peel the other onion and the carrots.

3. Cut the onion in half and the carrots into 4 lengthwise.

4. Peel the potatoes and cut into chunks. Boil with the prepared onion and carrots and the celery, until the potatoes are tender.

5. Put on your rubber gloves and wash the nettle tops in cold water.

6. Drain the cooking water from the potatoes into a pan and add the washed nettles.

7. Bring to the boil and simmer for 5 minutes. Drain, and retain the cooking liquid.

8. Mash the potatoes, discarding the carrot, onion and celery.

9. Combine the fried onions with the potatoes and nettles. Add some of the cooking liquid and whizz in the processor. Add more cooking liquid as needed.

10. Transfer to a pan and heat through – don't boil as this will impair the flavour.

11. Check for seasoning: you may need a little salt and pepper.

12. Serve with crusty bread, with croutons and fried bacon pieces scattered over the top.

Note: Towards the end of the picking season, the nettles develop a more intense taste. Stir in a little cream or crème fraîche to balance the flavour.

Roasted Red Pepper and Tomato Soup

You can turn this into a lovely summer lunch served with thick slices of mozzarella, some olives and fresh basil, and plenty of crusty bread.

Serves 4

2 large onions

1–2 finely chopped garlic cloves

Olive oil

4 large red peppers

Basil leaves

½ sliced red chilli, or to taste (optional)

2 x 500g cartons passata

Squeeze of tomato purée

Salt and freshly ground black pepper

To serve

Crusty bread, fresh basil leaves

1. Prepare and slice the onions and fry gently until soft and golden, adding the garlic towards the end of the cooking time.

2. Halve and de-seed the peppers.

3. Put the peppers cut side down on an oiled baking tray. Drizzle with a little more oil and scatter with basil leaves.

4. Roast for 20–30 minutes or until they are soft and the skins are just starting to blacken.

5. Once the peppers are roasted, discard the basil leaves and put the peppers in a sealed plastic bag for a few minutes.

6. As soon as the peppers have cooled, remove the skins.

7. Put the peppers into the processor bowl with the fried onions and garlic and the chilli, if using, and whizz.

8. Add one carton of passata and the tomato purée to the pepper mixture.

9. Whizz until smooth.

10. Transfer to a clean pan, stir in the second carton of passata and heat through – don't boil as this will impair the flavour.

11. Check for seasoning: you may need a little salt and pepper.

12. Serve with crusty bread and garnish with fresh basil leaves.

Main Meal Chicken and Potato Soup

This is like the traditional meat and two veg but in a soup. It's a tasty soup that everyone will enjoy, but is particularly soothing and nourishing for invalids and anyone recovering from an illness.

Serves 4

2 large onions

Either 2 chicken breasts, 4 chicken thighs or 1 chicken breast quarter, skin removed

2 carrots

4 medium-sized potatoes

3–4 sticks of celery

A few sprigs of parsley, including stalks, if available

Salt and freshly ground black pepper

To serve

Crusty bread

Tips

- Add a handful of frozen mixed vegetables before the final heating through.

- As with the **Leek and Potato Soup** (page 58) try adding a dash of dry (but not extra dry) vermouth to the soup at the final heating through for an intriguing herbal flavour, but go easy as too much can be overpowering. In early nineteenth-century France, vermouth was viewed as medicine.

1. Peel and slice one of the onions and fry gently until soft and golden.

2. Fry the chicken pieces until fully cooked and the juices run clear.

3. Peel the other onion and the carrots.

4. Cut the onion in half and the carrots into 4 lengthwise. Cut each celery stick into quarters.

5. Peel the potatoes and cut into chunks. Boil with the prepared onion, carrots, celery and parsley, until the potatoes are tender.

6. Strain the cooked potatoes and other vegetables and reserve the cooking water. Remove the onion, celery and parsley and discard.

7. Mash the potatoes and carrots together and put into the processor bowl with the fried onion.

8. Shred or dice the chicken.

9. Reserve half of the prepared chicken and add the rest to the processor bowl.

10. Whizz together until smooth, adding more cooking water as needed.

11. Transfer to a clean pan and stir in the remaining chicken meat.

12. Heat through – don't boil as this will impair the flavour – and add more liquid if required.

13. Check for seasoning: you may need a little salt and pepper.

14. Serve with crusty bread.

Chapter 7

Delicious Cakes and Muffins

Use the normal blade attachment of your processor for all the recipes in this chapter.

Cakes are just so easy in a food processor. All you do is add your ingredients to the food processor bowl, whizz until smooth and bake in the correct tin for the right amount of time at the right temperature.

The basic Victoria sandwich mixture, often so difficult to get right by hand, is so straightforward with this method. Mastering the Victoria sandwich then opens up the way for light and fluffy chocolate and coffee cakes, cupcakes, and fairy and butterfly cakes as they are all variations on the same theme.

Food processors are also fabulous for whizzing up the accompanying glacé and buttercream icings: not only is it quicker in the processor but also, since there is no need to sieve the icing sugar (a few turns in the processor will eliminate any lumps), neither you nor your work surfaces will be covered in clouds of sweet, choking dust. You can even make marzipan in your food processor: it's incredibly quick and much better than anything ready-made.

General Pointers for Cake Making

- Use butter rather than margarine for superior flavour and texture and 'mouth feel'.

- Soften the butter beforehand – try microwaving on High for 10–20 seconds.

- Self-raising flour can sometimes give disappointing results: it may be past or nearing its sell-by date or it may have been stored badly, and the raising agents within the flour may have lost their effectiveness. Play safe and add your own raising agents to plain flour, in the amounts specified in each recipe.

- The majority of cakes in this book are of the 'light and fluffy' variety. For maximum fluffiness the raising agents, cream of tartar and bicarbonate of soda, are added to these recipes in combination at a ratio of 2:1.

- Sieve your flour and raising agents together into the food processor bowl – both to introduce air and to ensure the raising agents are evenly mixed throughout the flour.

- Ideally, eggs and milk should be at room temperature – in contrast to pastry making, where ingredients should be cold, the ingredients for cakes should be warm.

- Eggs should be as fresh as possible for optimum rising and performance.

- Oven temperature and timing are crucial: individual ovens vary tremendously in performance so, for example, in a fierce fan oven, 18 minutes at 160°C may be ideal for a Victoria sandwich but a slower oven may bake it to perfection in 22 minutes at 180°C or even 190°C on the dial. Get to know your oven and keep notes for future reference.

Classic Victoria Sandwich

This beautiful classic cake is the master recipe for all your other light sponge cakes. Rather than adding all the ingredients together in an 'all-in-one' method, for best results the ingredients are added in the order they would be if mixed by hand.

Cuts into 8 slices

175g (6oz) butter, softened

175g (6oz) caster sugar

175g (6oz) plain flour

1 level tsp bicarbonate of soda

2 level tsp cream of tartar

3 medium eggs

2 tablespoons milk

Raspberry jam, ideally seedless, and icing sugar to finish

You will need 2 greased 18cm (7in) loose-bottomed sandwich tins

1. Preheat the oven to (160–180°C fan ovens) or equivalent – 160°C may be preferable in fierce ovens

2. Whizz the butter and sugar together in the processor until light and fluffy.

3. Add the raising agents to the weighed flour and sieve half carefully into the food processor bowl, completely covering the butter and sugar mixture.

4. Add the eggs and the rest of the flour and whizz to mix.

5. Add the milk and whizz until smooth and glossy. You may need to scrape the mixture down from the sides a couple of times with a flexible spatula.

6. Pour into the prepared cake tins.

7. Bake for 18–20 minutes or until risen and golden and a skewer inserted comes out clean.

8. Allow to rest for a few moments then carefully loosen the edges with a small palette knife.

9. Transfer to a cooling rack using a large palette knife to loosen the bottoms.

10. Once the cakes are cool, spread one with jam and set the other on top.

11. Dust with icing sugar just before serving: stir it through a tea strainer for even distribution.

Fairy Cakes and Cupcakes

Use the Victoria sandwich recipe for fairy cakes and cupcakes. The mixture is sufficient for approximately 18 fairy cakes or 12 cupcakes.

1. Make the mixture as before and bake at the same temperature for approximately 14–15 minutes for fairy cakes and 18–22 minutes for cupcakes.

2. Use muffin or tart tins lined with standard cake cases for the fairy cakes and a muffin tin lined with paper muffin cases for the cupcakes.

3. Top with buttercream or glacé icing.

Tip
*   You can also make teeny, tiny mini fairy cakes with this mixture. You will need 2 x mini-muffin tins and up to 24 *petits fours* cases. Make up a half quantity of mixture and bake for around 10 minutes or until risen and pale golden and springy to the touch.

Lemon Glacé Icing

Use lemon juice rather than water to mix your icing: it will take the edge off the sweetness and give a lovely fresh flavour.

75g (3oz) icing sugar

Approximately 1–2 tbsp lemon juice

½ tsp glycerine

1. Tip the icing sugar into the clean, dry food processor and whizz to eliminate any lumps.

2. Add 2 tablespoons of juice and whizz until smooth.

3. Add a drop more juice if necessary.

4. Finally, add the glycerine and whizz again until smooth and glossy.

5. Once the cakes are cold, top each one with a teaspoonful of icing.

Butterfly Cakes

Make the original Victoria sandwich mix as before and once the cakes are cool slice the tops off and put to one side.

1. Spoon a little dab of buttercream onto each cake.

2. Cut each top in half so you have two 'wings' and arrange on top of each cake.

3. Just before you want to eat the cakes, sieve some icing sugar over the top as the finishing touch.

Lemon and Vanilla Buttercream

The lemon and vanilla combined give the most beautiful flavour.

175g (6oz) icing sugar

75g (3oz) butter, softened

¼ – ½ tsp vanilla extract

Squeeze of lemon juice

1. Tip the icing sugar into the clean, dry food processor and whizz to eliminate any lumps.

2. Add the softened butter and vanilla extract and whizz until fully mixed.

3. Add the lemon juice to loosen the mixture slightly and whizz until smooth.

Chocolate Cake

This is virtually the same as the Victoria sandwich mix but with cocoa replacing some of the flour.

Cuts into 8 slices

175g (6oz) butter, softened

175g (6oz) caster sugar

150g (5oz) plain flour

1 level tsp bicarbonate of soda

2 level tsp cream of tartar

25g (1oz) cocoa powder

3 medium eggs

2 tbsp milk

Chocolate buttercream to finish

1. You will need 2 greased 18cm (7in) loose-bottomed sandwich tins

2. Preheat the oven to 180°C (fan ovens) or equivalent – 160°C may be preferable in fierce ovens.

3. Whizz the butter and sugar together in the processor until light and fluffy.

4. Add the raising agents and cocoa to the weighed flour and sieve half carefully into the food processor bowl, completely covering the butter and sugar mixture.

5. Add the eggs and the rest of the flour and whizz to mix.

6. Add the milk and whizz until smooth and glossy. You may need to scrape the mixture down from the sides a couple of times with a flexible spatula.

7. Pour into the prepared cake tins.

8. Bake for 18–20 minutes or until risen and a skewer inserted comes out clean.

9. Allow to rest for a few moments then carefully loosen the edges with a small palette knife.

10. Transfer to a cooling rack using a large palette knife to loosen the bottoms.

11. Spread some of the buttercream carefully onto one of the sponges with a small palette knife, sit the second sponge on top and spread the rest of the buttercream over it.

Tip
- Use actual cocoa, not drinking chocolate.

Chocolate Buttercream

25g (1oz) good-quality cocoa powder

150g (5oz) icing sugar

75g (3oz) butter, softened

A little milk to mix

1. Tip the combined cocoa and icing sugar into the clean, dry food processor and whizz to eliminate any lumps.

2. Add the softened butter and whizz until fully mixed.

3. Add the milk to loosen the mixture slightly and whizz until smooth.

Chocolate Fairy Cakes and Cupcakes

You can use the chocolate sponge recipe for chocolate fairy cakes and cupcakes. The mixture is sufficient for approximately 18 fairy cakes or 12 cupcakes.

1. Make the mixture as before and bake at the same temperature for approximately 14–15 minutes for fairy cakes and 18–22 minutes for cupcakes.

2. Use muffin or tart tins lined with standard cake cases for the fairy cakes and a muffin tin lined with paper muffin cases for the cupcakes.

3. Top with chocolate buttercream or glacé icing.

Chocolate Glacé Icing

50g (2oz) icing sugar

25g (1oz) cocoa powder

Approximately 1–2 tbsp milk

½ tsp glycerine

1. Put the icing sugar and cocoa into the clean, dry bowl of your food processor and give it a few turns to eliminate any lumps.

2. Add the milk and whizz until smooth.

3. Add a drop more milk if necessary.

4. Finally, add the glycerine and whizz again until smooth and glossy.

Chocolate Butterfly Cakes

Make the original chocolate cake mix as before and once the cakes are cool slice the tops off and put to one side.

1. Spoon a little dab of chocolate buttercream onto each cake.

2. Cut each top in half so you have two 'wings' and arrange on top of each cake.

3. Just before you want to eat them, you may like to sieve some icing sugar over the top as the finishing touch.

Coffee Cake

Your food processor will make short work of this traditional favourite. Again it is virtually the same as the Victoria sandwich mix but with added coffee powder.

Cuts into 8 slices

175g (6oz) butter, softened

175g (6oz) caster sugar

175g (6oz) plain flour

1 level tsp bicarbonate of soda

2 level tsp cream of tartar

2 tsp instant espresso coffee powder

3 medium eggs

2 tbsp milk

Coffee buttercream to finish

You will need 2 greased 18cm (7in) loose-bottomed sandwich tins

1. Preheat the oven to 180°C (fan ovens) or equivalent – 160°C may be preferable in fierce ovens.

2. Whizz the butter and sugar together in the processor until light and fluffy.

3. Add the raising agents and coffee powder to the weighed flour and sieve half carefully into the food processor bowl, completely covering the butter and sugar mixture.

4. Add the eggs and the rest of the flour and whizz to mix.

5. Add the milk and whizz until smooth and glossy. You may need to scrape the mixture down from the sides a couple of times with a flexible spatula.

6. Pour into the prepared cake tins.

7. Bake for 18–20 minutes or until risen and golden and a skewer inserted comes out clean.

8. Allow to rest for a few moments then carefully loosen the edges with a small palette knife.

9. Transfer to a cooling rack using a large palette knife to loosen the bottoms.

10. Once cool, spread the buttercream over one of the sponges and set the other on top. You may like to sift a little icing sugar over the top just before serving.

11. Alternatively, sandwich the cake with coffee buttercream and ice with coffee glacé icing. Decorate with walnut halves or chocolate buttons.

Coffee Buttercream

2 tsp instant espresso coffee powder

1–2 tbsp hot water

175g (6oz) icing sugar

75g (3oz) butter, softened

1. Dissolve the coffee powder in 1–2 tablespoons of hot water and set aside.

2. Tip the icing sugar into the clean, dry food processor and whizz to eliminate any lumps.

3. Add the softened butter and whizz until fully mixed.

4. Add the disolved coffee and whizz until smooth.

Coffee Fairy Cakes and Cupcakes

You can use the coffee sponge recipe for coffee fairy cakes and cupcakes. The mixture is sufficient for approximately 18 fairy cakes or 12 cupcakes.

1. Make the mixture as before and bake at the same temperature for approximately 14–15 minutes for fairy cakes and 18–22 minutes for cupcakes.

2. Use muffin or tart tins lined with standard cake cases for the fairy cakes and a muffin tin lined with paper muffin cases for the cupcakes.

3. Top with coffee buttercream or glacé icing.

Coffee Glacé Icing

75g (3oz) icing sugar

2 tsp instant espresso coffee powder

Approximately 2 tbsp hot water

½ tsp glycerine

1. Put the icing sugar into the clean, dry bowl of your food processor and give it a few turns to eliminate any lumps.

2. Dissolve the coffee powder in 1–2 tablespoons of hot water.

3. Add the dissolved coffee to the icing sugar and whizz until smooth.

4. Add a drop more water if necessary.

5. Finally, add the glycerine and whizz again until smooth and glossy.

Coffee Butterfly Cakes

1. Make the original coffee cake mix as before and once the cakes are cool slice the tops off and put to one side.

2. Spoon a little dab of coffee buttercream onto each cake.

3. Cut each top in half so you have two 'wings' and arrange on top of each cake.

4. Just before you want to eat them, you may like to sieve some icing sugar over the top as the finishing touch.

Madeira Cake

Here is a lovely old-fashioned cake, plain and not at all fancy. The lemon zest gives a fresh taste to the cake but leave it out if you prefer.

Cuts into 8 slices

110g (4oz) butter, softened

110g (4oz) caster sugar

175g (6oz) plain flour

1 level tsp bicarbonate of soda

2 level tsp cream of tartar

2 medium eggs

Grated zest of 1 lemon (optional)

2 tbsp milk

You will need a greased 18cm (7in) round loose-bottomed cake tin

1. Preheat the oven to 160°C (fan ovens) or equivalent.

2. Whizz the butter and sugar together until combined and fluffy.

3. Add the raising agents to the weighed flour and sieve half carefully into the food processor bowl, completely covering the butter and sugar mixture.

4. Add the eggs and the rest of the flour with the lemon zest, if using.

5. Whizz briefly, and add the milk.

6. Whizz until everything is mixed together but not overmixed. You may need to stop the machine a couple of times and scrape the mixture down from the sides.

7. Pour into the prepared tin and bake for 40–50 minutes, until risen and golden and a skewer inserted comes out clean.

8. Leave in the tin to settle and contract away from the sides for a few moments then transfer to a wire rack until completely cold.

9. Once cold, store in an airtight tin.

Tips
- Madeira, Seed, Coconut and Lemon Drizzle cakes can be baked in either a greased 18cm (7in) round loose-bottomed cake tin or a greased and lined 450g (1lb) loaf tin (see Lemon Drizzle lining tip on page 86). Both tin sizes use the same oven temperature and timings.

- Alternatively, all can be baked as little cupcakes or muffins in a 12-cup muffin tin lined with paper muffin cases. Bake for 18–22 minutes at 160°C (fan ovens) or equivalent.

Seed Cake

You can make a lovely old-fashioned seed cake using the Madeira cake mix. Simply make the cake as above but leave out the lemon zest and add instead **2 tbsp caraway seeds**. Add the seeds at the very end: remove the food processor blade and stir them in so they remain unbroken.

Coconut Cake

This is a lovely moist cake.

Cuts into 8 slices

110g (4oz) butter, softened

110g (4oz) caster sugar

110g (4oz) plain flour

1 level tsp bicarbonate of soda

2 level tsp cream of tartar

2 eggs

2 tbsp milk

50g (2oz) desiccated coconut

You will need a greased 18cm (7in) round loose-bottomed cake tin

1. Preheat the oven to 160°C (fan ovens) or equivalent.

2. Whizz the butter and sugar together until combined and fluffy.

3. Add the raising agents to the weighed flour and sieve half carefully into the food processor bowl, completely covering the butter and sugar mixture.

4. Add the eggs and the rest of the flour.

5. Whizz briefly, and add the milk.

6. Whizz until everything is mixed together but not overmixed. You may need to stop the machine a couple of times and scrape the mixture down from the sides.

7. Finally, add the coconut and whizz briefly to mix it all in evenly.

8. Pour into the prepared tin and bake for 40–45 minutes, until risen and golden and a skewer inserted comes out clean.

9. Leave in the tin to settle and contract away from the sides for a few moments then transfer to a wire rack until completely cold.

10. Once cold, store in an airtight tin.

Tip
- Remember, raspberry jam and coconut together is a fantastic flavour combination. You could split a full-size coconut cake and sandwich the halves together with jam, or slice the tops off coconut fairy cakes or cupcakes and turn them into 'jam and coconut butterfly cakes'.

Lemon Drizzle Cake

This is a classic teatime lemon drizzle cake: moist and light, not too sweet and not too sharp.

Cuts into 8 slices

For the cake

110g (4oz) butter, softened

110g (4oz) caster sugar

175g (6oz) plain flour

1 level tsp bicarbonate of soda

2 level tsp cream of tartar

2 medium eggs, beaten

Grated zest of 1 lemon

2 tbsp milk

For the drizzle

Juice of 2 lemons and 2 level tbsp
  caster sugar

You will need a greased and lined
450g (1lb) loaf tin

1. Preheat the oven to 160°C (fan ovens) or equivalent.

2. Whizz the butter and sugar together until combined and fluffy.

3. Add the raising agents to the weighed flour and sieve half carefully into the food processor bowl, completely covering the butter and sugar mixture.

4. Add the eggs and the rest of the flour with the lemon zest.

5. Whizz briefly, and add the milk.

6. Whizz until everything is smooth and glossy. You may need to stop the machine a couple of times and scrape the mixture down from the sides.

7. Pour into the prepared tin and bake for 40–45 minutes, until risen and golden and a skewer inserted comes out clean.

8. While the cake is baking, heat the lemon juice and sugar together in a small heavy-bottomed saucepan, stirring frequently until the sugar has dissolved. Put aside to cool.

9. When the cake is baked, leave it in its tin and, while still warm, prick the surface lightly and spoon the drizzle evenly all over the top.

10. Leave the cake in the tin until it is completely cold and the drizzle has soaked in.

11. Once cold, transfer to an airtight container and use within a couple of days.

Tip
- Line your loaf tin with a strip of double thickness greaseproof paper from end to end, with the paper ends sticking up: this will enable you to lift the loaf out easily.

Apple and Cinnamon Cake

The enticing fragrance and warm taste complement the apple beautifully in this delicious autumnal cake.

Makes 12 squares

110g (4oz) butter, softened

110g (4oz) caster sugar

175g (6oz) plain flour

1 level tsp bicarbonate of soda

2 level tsp cream of tartar

1 level tsp powdered cinnamon

2 eggs

50g (2oz) ground almonds

175g (6oz) apple, peeled and finely chopped

Plus: an additional 50g (2oz) apple, peeled and diced

You will need a greased 18cm (7in) loose-bottomed cake tin

1. Preheat the oven to 160°C (fan oven) or equivalent.

2. Whizz the butter and sugar together in the processor.

3. Add the raising agents and cinnamon to the weighed flour and sieve half over the butter mixture, covering it completely. Add the eggs and the rest of the flour and whizz to mix.

4. Add the ground almonds and whizz again.

5. Add the chopped apple and whizz until the mixture is fully combined, smooth and glossy.

6. Remove the processor blade, scrape any mixture back into the bowl and stir in the 50g (2oz) of diced apple.

7. Spoon into the prepared tin, cover loosely with greaseproof paper and bake for about 40–45 minutes, or until a skewer inserted comes out clean. Leave to settle for a few moments then remove from the tin and finish cooling on a wire rack.

Iced Banana Loaf

The lemon and vanilla glacé icing complements the banana cake beautifully but it's equally good served plain.

Cuts into 8 slices

110g (4oz) butter, softened

110g (4oz) caster sugar

175g (6oz) plain flour

2 level tsp cream of tartar

1 level tsp bicarbonate of soda

2 medium eggs

50g (2oz) ground almonds

150–175g (5–6oz) ripe bananas (but no more or the cake will be heavy), peeled weight, mashed to a purée but not liquidy

You will need a greased 450g (1lb) loaf tin lined with a strip of greaseproof paper

1. Preheat the oven to 160°C (fan oven) or equivalent.

2. Whizz the butter and sugar together in a food processor until soft and fluffy.

3. Add the raising agents to the weighed flour and sieve half over the butter mixture covering it completely. Add the eggs and the rest of the flour and whizz to mix.

4. Add the ground almonds and whizz again.

5. Finally, add the banana and whizz until smooth and fully mixed.

6. Spoon into the prepared tin and bake for about 40 minutes, or until a skewer inserted into the cake comes out clean.

7. Leave in the tin to settle for a few moments then remove and cool on a wire rack.

Tip
- Line your loaf tin with a strip of double thickness greaseproof paper from end to end, with the paper ends sticking up: this will enable you to lift the loaf out easily.

Lemon and Vanilla Glacé Icing

The lemon and vanilla flavours work well together and with the banana. Don't add too much vanilla as it can be overpowering. The consistency of the icing should be fairly thick and spreadable rather than runny.

75g (3oz) icing sugar

Approximately 1–2 tbsp lemon juice

¼–½ tsp vanilla extract

½ tsp glycerine

1. Put the icing sugar into the clean, dry bowl of your processor and give it a few turns to eliminate any lumps.

2. Add the lemon juice and vanilla extract and whizz until smooth. Add a drop more juice if necessary.

3. Finally, add the glycerine and whizz again until smooth and glossy.

4. Spread over the top of the cooled banana loaf.

5. Store in an airtight tin.

Tips

- Iced Banana Loaf, Apple and Cinnamon, Carrot, Courgette, Strawberry and Orange and Almond cakes can all be baked in either a greased 18cm (7in) round loose-bottomed cake tin or a greased and lined 450g (1lb) loaf tin (see Iced Banana Loaf lining tip opposite). Both tin sizes use the same oven temperature and timings.

- Alternatively, all can be baked as little cupcakes or muffins in a 12-cup muffin tin lined with paper muffin cases. Bake for 18–22 minutes at 160°C (fan ovens) or equivalent.

Carrot Cake

Carrot cake is always popular and so easy in the food processor. The cinnamon in this recipe gives a hint of warmth and depth, the orange zest a lovely freshness and the orange buttercream icing a touch of luxury.

Cuts into 8 slices

110g (4oz) butter, softened

110g (4oz) caster sugar

150g (5oz) grated carrot (grated weight)

Zest of 1 orange, finely grated

110g (4oz) wholemeal flour

50g (2oz) plain flour

1 level tsp bicarbonate of soda

2 level tsp cream of tartar

1 tsp ground cinnamon

50g (2oz) ground almonds

2 medium eggs

You will need an 18cm (7in) greased loose-bottomed cake tin

1. Preheat the oven to 160°C (fan oven) or equivalent.

2. Whizz the butter and sugar together in a food processor.

3. Add the grated carrot and orange zest and whizz again.

4. Add the flours, raising agents, cinnamon, ground almonds and eggs and whizz until combined.

5. Spoon into the prepared tin and bake for about 40–45 minutes, or until a skewer inserted into the cake comes out clean.

6. Leave in the tin for a few moments then loosen the sides and bottom with a palette knife, remove from the tin and cool on a wire rack.

Orange Buttercream Icing

This makes a delicious change from the usual cream cheese frosting.

110g (4oz) icing sugar

50g (2oz) butter, softened

Squeeze of orange juice

1. Tip the icing sugar into the clean, dry food processor and whizz to eliminate any lumps.

2. Add the softened butter and whizz until fully mixed.

3. Add a squeeze of orange juice to loosen the mixture slightly and whizz until smooth.

Courgette Cake

The courgette works in a similar way to carrot to add moistness and volume to the cake but has a much more delicate flavour. The courgette seems to extend the keeping qualities as well.

Cuts into 8 slices

150g (5oz) peeled courgette, cut into short lengths

110g (4oz) butter, softened

110g (4oz) caster sugar

Finely grated zest of 1½ lemons

175g (6oz) plain flour

1 level tsp bicarbonate soda

2 level tsp cream of tartar

2 medium eggs, beaten

1 tsp vanilla extract

50g (2oz) ground almonds

You will need a greased 18cm (7in) loose-bottomed cake tin

1. Preheat the oven to 160°C (fan oven) or equivalent.

2. Whizz the prepared courgette into strands.

3. Add the butter, sugar and lemon zest and whizz until combined.

4. Add the raising agents to the weighed flour and sieve half of it over the mixture.

5. Add the eggs and vanilla and sieve in the rest of the flour and raising agents.

6. Whizz briefly and add the ground almonds. Whizz until smooth and well mixed.

7. Spoon into the prepared tin and bake for about 40–45 minutes, or until a skewer inserted into the cake comes out clean.

8. Allow to settle for a few moments then remove and cool on a wire rack.

Strawberry Cake

This beautiful summery cake is slightly unusual in that strawberries are incorporated into the cake mixture itself.

Cuts into 8 slices

110g (4oz) softened butter

110g (4oz) caster sugar

175g (6oz) plain flour

2 level teaspoons cream of tartar

1 level teaspoon bicarbonate of soda

50g (2oz) ground almonds

2 medium eggs, beaten

A few drops of vanilla extract

175g (6oz) hulled strawberries, sliced

1. Preheat the oven to 160°C (fan ovens) or equivalent.

2. Whizz the butter and sugar together in a food processor.

3. Add the raising agents to the weighed flour and sieve half of it over the mixture. Add the eggs and vanilla.

4. Add the rest of the flour and the ground almonds. Whizz again.

5. Add the strawberries and whizz until they are all pulped and incorporated into the mixture: the mixture should now be dusky pink with the odd speck of strawberry.

6. Spoon into the prepared tin and bake for about 40–45 minutes, or until a skewer inserted into the cake comes out clean.

7. Loosen the sides and bottom with a palette knife, remove from the tin and cool on a wire rack.

Orange and Almond Cake

This lovely and unusual cake keeps well in a tin for up to a week, becoming moister and more flavourful.

Cuts into 8 slices

2 oranges, not too large: about 150g (5oz) pulped fruit is ideal

110g (4oz) butter, softened

110g (4oz) caster sugar

110g (4oz) plain flour

2 level tsp cream of tartar

1 level tsp bicarbonate of soda

110g (4oz) ground almonds

2 medium eggs, beaten

You will need a greased 18cm (7in) loose-bottomed cake tin

1. Preheat the oven to 160°C (fan oven) or equivalent.

2. Take one of the oranges and put it whole and unpeeled into a pan of cold water. Bring to the boil and simmer, partially covered, for about 30–45 minutes or until it is soft.

3. Cool the orange and cut into several pieces. Remove any pips and central pith, and any bits of membrane that will come away easily. Put the rest into your processor bowl and whizz to a fairly smooth, pale, orange-flecked purée.

4. Peel or grate all the zest from the second orange (a lemon zester works best) and add to the purée.

5. Add the butter and sugar and whizz until smooth.

6. Add the raising agents to the weighed flour.

7. Add the flour and raising agents, the ground almonds and eggs to the mixture and whizz until smooth and thoroughly mixed.

8. Pour the mixture into the prepared tin.

9. Bake for about 40–45 minutes, or until golden on top, firm to the touch, and a skewer inserted comes out clean.

10. Loosen the sides and bottom with a palette knife, remove from tin and cool on a wire rack. Eat warm or cold.

Tip
- Serve with a dollop of Greek yoghurt as a pudding or for a weekend breakfast.

Light Cheesy Muffins

These savoury light and fluffy muffins are gorgeous fresh from the oven, just as they are, or cold with a little soft butter.

Makes 12 muffins

110g (4oz) butter, softened

10g (½oz) caster sugar

225g (8oz) plain flour

2 level tsp cream of tartar

1 level tsp bicarbonate of soda

Good pinch mustard powder – around ½ tsp

Small pinch salt

2 medium eggs

4 tbsp milk

75g (3oz) well-flavoured mature Cheddar cheese, grated

You will need a greased 12-cup muffin tin lined with paper muffin cases

1. Preheat the oven to 160°C (fan oven) or equivalent.

2. Whizz the butter and sugar together in a food processor.

3. Add the raising agents, mustard and salt to the weighed flour and sieve half over the butter mixture, covering it completely.

4. Add the eggs and the rest of the flour and whizz to mix.

5. Add the milk and whizz again.

6. Add the cheese. Whizz until combined: the mixture will remain fairly stiff.

7. Spoon into the muffin cases, dividing the mixture as equally as possible.

8. Bake for about 15 minutes, or until the muffins are springy to the touch and a skewer inserted comes out clean.

9. Leave in the tin to settle for a few minutes then transfer to a wire rack.

10. Cover with a clean tea towel to keep the muffins moist and prevent them drying out as they cool.

Tips
- For a cheesier flavour use a stronger-flavoured cheese or include a little grated Parmesan in the recommended weight of cheese. Avoid adding more than 75g (3oz) cheese overall as the muffins may become heavy and greasy.

- To avoid the mustard powder clumping together, sieve over the flour through a tea strainer.

Cheese and Courgette Muffins

These extra-light, savoury muffins are surprisingly child-friendly: it's very hard to tell they contain courgette beyond the merest green fleck and a lovely light moistness.

Makes 12 muffins

175g (6oz) courgettes, peeled and cut into short lengths

110g (4oz) butter, softened

10g (½oz) caster sugar

225g (8oz) plain flour

2 level tsp cream of tartar

1 level tsp bicarbonate of soda

½ tsp mustard powder (or to taste)

Small pinch of salt

2 medium eggs

75g (3oz) well-flavoured mature Cheddar cheese, grated

You will need a greased 12-cup muffin tin lined with paper muffin cases

1. Preheat the oven to 160°C (fan oven) or equivalent.

2. Whizz the prepared courgettes into short strands, add the butter and sugar and whizz until fluffy.

3. Add the raising agents, mustard and salt to the weighed flour and sieve half over the butter mixture, covering it completely.

4. Add the eggs and the rest of the flour and whizz to mix.

5. Add the cheese. Whizz until combined: the mixture will remain fairly stiff.

6. Spoon into the prepared tin, dividing the mixture as equally as possible among the muffin cases.

7. Bake for about 15–20 minutes, or until the muffins are springy to the touch and a skewer inserted comes out clean.

8. Leave in the tin to settle for a few minutes then transfer to a wire rack.

9. Cover with a clean tea towel to keep the muffins moist and prevent them drying out as they cool.

Tip
- If seeds have begun to form in the courgettes, cut them lengthways and use a teaspoon to scrape out the seedy bits.

Cornmeal Muffins

These cheerful yellow-coloured light cornmeal muffins are delicious with soup or chilli. Alternatively, serve them for breakfast with a drizzle of honey. Eat them fresh from the oven just as they are or cold with a little soft butter.

Makes 12 muffins

110g (4oz) butter, softened

10g (½oz) caster sugar

175g (6oz) plain flour

2 level tsp cream of tartar

1 level tsp bicarbonate of soda

Small pinch of salt

2 medium eggs

50g fine cornmeal

4 tbsp milk

You will need a greased 12-cup muffin tin lined with paper muffin cases

1. Preheat the oven to 160°C (fan oven) or equivalent.

2. Whizz the butter and sugar together in a food processor.

3. Add the raising agents and salt to the weighed flour and sieve half over the butter mixture, covering it completely.

4. Add the eggs.

5. Sieve the rest of the flour and raising agents and the cornmeal over the eggs and whizz briefly.

6. Add the milk and whizz again.

7. Spoon into the prepared tin, dividing the mixture as equally as possible.

8. Bake for about 15 minutes, or until the buns are springy to the touch and a skewer inserted comes out clean.

9. Leave in the tin to settle for a few minutes then transfer to a wire rack.

10. Cover with a clean tea towel to keep the muffins moist and prevent them drying out as they cool.

Red Hot Chilli Muffins

You can make chilli versions of all of the above savoury muffins.

Make the muffins as before, adding ¼–½ **tsp chilli powder** to the dry ingredients at the beginning and proceed as for the main recipe.

Alternatively, fry **fresh red chilli** (amount to taste) in **a small amount of oil**, drain briefly on kitchen paper and add at the end of any of the recipes. One advantage of using fresh chillies is that they show up attractively in the finished muffins. Again, proceed as for the main recipe.

Slightly Restrained Elevenses Brownie

This is not a super-duper luxury brownie oozing with fabulously rich chocolate; it is more of a restrained affair suitable for a treat with a cup of coffee or tea. It is also popular with children. Some brownies can be a bit tooth-achingly sweet: this recipe makes a less sweet, less rich brownie with a lovely deep chocolatey flavour.

Makes 16 squares

175g (6oz) butter, softened

175g (6oz) caster sugar

75g (3oz) self-raising flour

3 eggs, lightly beaten

25g (1oz) good-quality cocoa powder

50g (2oz) ground almonds

2 tbsp milk

1. You will need a greased 20cm (8in) square brownie tin

2. Preheat oven to 160°C (fan oven) or equivalent.

3. Whiz the softened butter and sugar together until combined and fluffy. Sieve in a little flour and add the eggs. Add the rest of the flour, the cocoa powder, the ground almonds and milk. Whiz until smooth, stopping a couple of times to scrape the mixture down from the sides.

4. Remove the blade and scrape into the prepared tin, easing it into the corners.

5. Bake for approximately 25 minutes; depending on your oven it could be a fraction less or a little more. A skewer inserted should *just* show very slight traces of mixture.

6. Mark into squares and cool in the tin: if you are worried about scratching your tin, use a sturdy plastic picnic knife. Cover with a clean tea towel to keep the brownies moist as they cool. Store in an airtight tin when completely cold.

Chapter 8

Making Pastry

You need a light touch and cool hands for successful hand-made shortcrust pastry. Happily, your food processor can provide you with the lightness of touch. Here's how to make terrific pastry with a food processor:

- Make sure your ingredients are cold.

- Whizz the flour and fat together briefly into fine crumbs.

- If making sweet pastry, add the sugar and whizz briefly to mix.

- Add the required amount of cold water.

- Whizz until the pastry forms large crumbs but is still not totally combined.

- Remove the pastry from the processor and form gently into a ball by hand.

- Your pastry is now ready to roll without resting or chilling.

- The final point to bear in mind is: always roll gently on a lightly floured board with a lightly floured rolling pin, usually to a thickness of a little less than a pound coin. If you use too much flour for rolling it will get into your pastry, making it crack and break; plus, you are in effect upping the flour to fat ratio, which makes the pastry less 'melt in the mouth'.

Beware!
If you process the pastry until it comes together in a large ball, it will still be useable but slightly tougher and not quite as crumbly and delicious as when it is finished by hand.

If you carry on processing beyond the ball stage the pastry will become overprocessed and unworkable.

No stretching!
It is really important that you don't stretch the pastry when lining the baking tins: if you do, it will ping back down the sides of the tins during baking, like overstretched elastic, and shrink.

The amount of pastry given by the basic pastry recipes corresponds with the amount needed for all of the recipes in this book.

Use the normal blade attachment of your processor for all the recipes in this chapter.

Plain Shortcrust Pastry

This is your basic master recipe: all the other shortcrust pastry types covered in this book will be variations of this.

160g (6oz) plain flour

40g (1½oz) cold butter, diced

40g (1½oz) cold lard or block vegetable shortening, diced

Pinch of salt

2 tbsp cold water

1. Tip the flour into the bowl of your food processor and add the butter, lard or vegetable shortening and salt.

2. Whizz into fine crumbs.

3. Add the water and whizz again.

4. Once the mixture is starting to form big crumbs and clump together, turn it out onto a lightly floured board and knead it gently into a ball.

5. The pastry is now ready to use.

Mini Cheese Flans

These go down well at picnics and parties. There is no need to bake blind: as they are so small the filling and pastry can cook together.

Makes about 18

Plain Shortcrust Pastry

1 egg

1 egg yolk

Pinch of dry mustard powder

Freshly ground black or white pepper

6 tbsp cream (single or double, but not extra thick)

1 small onion, diced and fried in a little oil until soft and drained on kitchen paper

75g (3oz) cheese, grated

You will need 2 x 12-cup greased tart tins and a 6cm (2½in) plain cutter

1. Preheat the oven to 180°C (fan oven) or equivalent.

2. Roll the pastry gently with a lightly floured rolling pin on a floured board to the thickness of just less than a pound coin and cut into rounds. Press them gently into the tart tins.

3. Beat the egg and egg yolk with the mustard powder and pepper.

4. Add the cream and whisk until frothy and foamy.

5. Stir in the onion and cheese.

6. Spoon into the pastry cases.

7. Bake for approximately 14–15 minutes or until risen and golden. Serve warm or cold.

Tips

- If you are preparing some mini cheese flans for a party or special occasion and want to get ahead, try this: cut out all the flan cases and press them gently into the greased tart tins. Cover each tin completely with a large freezer bag, exclude all air and seal. Store them in the fridge for use next day (you can stack them on top of each other once they are in their separate bags). Make up your filling and store, covered, in the fridge overnight. Assemble and bake the next day.

- If you don't have enough tart tins to do this you can stack the cut-out flan cases in sealed freezer bags. Allow them time to come to room temperature before you fit them into the tins: the pastry will crack if it's too cold.

- You can also store the unbaked cases in the freezer.

Little Hot Chilli Pies

These are great for a warming winter tea by the fire or standing around in a cold garden on Guy Fawkes' night. Give them a chance to cool down a little before you bite into them as they retain the heat for quite a while after they have come out of the oven.

They are perfect to make with leftover chilli when you only have a small amount. You only need a heaped teaspoonful of chilli for each pie, so even if you make two batches, it's still not very much chilli! Make sure the chilli is well flavoured and not too sloppy.

It's more 'correct' to use plain cutters for savoury pies but the fluted ones do make these pies look very appealing.

Makes 12 pies

Plain Shortcrust Pastry

12 generous tsp leftover chilli

Approximately 25g grated Cheddar cheese (grated in a brisk up and down movement to avoid any long strands)

1. You will need 2 fluted cutters: $7\frac{1}{2}$cm (3in) and a 6cm ($2\frac{1}{2}$in), and a greased 12-cup tart tin.

2. Preheat the oven to 180°C (fan ovens) or equivalent.

3. Roll the pastry out gently with a floured rolling pin to a thickness of about $\frac{1}{2}$cm.

4. Cut out 12 circles with the larger cutter (for the pies) and 12 circles with the smaller cutter (for the lids). As you put the larger circles into the tart tins, firm them down gently to give the finished pies a good shape.

5. Put a generous teaspoon of chilli into each: don't overfill, though, as it can boil out. Brush the edge of each lid with water and press them gently onto the pies.

6. Top each pie with a little grated cheese, press the cheese down gently into the pastry.

7. Don't make a hole in the top with the point of a knife: the steam generated inside the pie will help to make sure the chilli is fully reheated and the tops of the pies will have an appealing domed shape. This won't happen if there is an escape hole in the lid.

8. Bake for about 15–18 minutes or until pale golden. Remove from the tin with a small palette knife and cool on a wire rack. Eat warm, not boiling hot.

Baked Bean Pies

These are fun for older children to make for a weekend or holiday tea but do be careful to let the pies cool down enough before you bite into them.

Makes 12 pies

Plain Shortcrust Pastry

415g tin baked beans

Approximately 25g grated Cheddar cheese (grated in a brisk up and down movement to avoid any long strands)

1. You will need 2 fluted cutters: 7½cm (3in) and a 6cm (2½in), and a greased 12-cup tart tin.

2. Preheat the oven to 180°C (fan oven) or equivalent.

3. Roll the pastry out gently with a floured rolling pin to a thickness of about ½ a centimetre.

4. Cut out 12 circles with the larger cutter (for the pies) and 12 circles with the smaller cutter (for the lids). As you put the larger circles into the tart tins, firm them down gently to give the finished pies a good shape.

5. Empty the tin of beans into a bowl and stir gently to make sure the sauce is distributed evenly. Put a about a level dessertspoon into each pie – you may not need the whole tin – you are aiming to fill each pie generously but not so much so that everything squelches out when you try to put the lids on.

6. Brush the edge of each lid with water and press them gently onto the pies.

7. Top each pie with a little grated cheese and press the cheese down gently into the pastry.

8. Don't make a hole in the top of the pies with the point of a knife: this will make the tops domed in shape rather than flat. They will be boiling hot inside when they first come out of the oven, so take care.

9. Bake for about 15–18 minutes or until pale golden. Remove from the tin with a small palette knife and cool on a wire rack. Eat warm, not boiling hot.

Variations
You can spice up the beans a bit if you like: try stirring in some curry paste or powder to taste and a few sultanas, or chilli powder or snipped fresh chilli. If you don't want to top the pies with cheese (maybe not with curried beans), you could glaze them instead with an egg beaten with a teaspoon of water.

Cheese Flan

Sometimes, you may prefer to make one large flan. This recipe uses the same quantities of Plain Shortcrust Pastry and filling as the mini flans. You will need to bake the pastry case blind first to avoid a 'soggy bottom'.

Cuts into 8 slices

Plain Shortcrust Pastry

1 egg

1 egg yolk

Pinch of dry mustard powder

Freshly ground black or white pepper

6 tbsp cream (single or double, but not extra thick)

1 small onion, diced and fried in a little oil until soft and drained on kitchen paper

75g (3oz) cheese, grated

You will need 2 x 12-cup greased tart tins and a 6cm (2½in) plain cutter

You will need a greased 20cm (8in) loose-bottomed flan tin, a circle of greaseproof paper to fit the flan tin and either dried pulses or ceramic baking beans

1. Preheat the oven to 180°C (fan oven) or equivalent.

2. Make up the pastry and filling as for the Mini Cheese Flans.

3. Take your ball of shortcrust and roll it gently into a large disc of just less than the thickness of a pound coin.

4. Roll it round your rolling pin and manoeuvre it gently on top of the prepared flan tin. Hold the sides upright while you settle it into the bottom of the tin, firming it gently with your fingers.

5. Trim away the excess.

6. Prick the bottom lightly all over with a fork.

7. Lay the circle of greaseproof paper on the bottom of the pastry case and fill it nearly to the top with baking beans.

8. Bake for 15–20 minutes.

9. Leave to settle for a few moments and remove the beans from the pastry case, taking care not to damage the edge of the pastry.

10. Reduce the oven temperature to 160°C (fan oven) or equivalent.

11. Pour in the filling and bake for a further 15–20 minutes or until the filling is risen and golden.

Tip
- Use the loose bottom of the flan tin as a template to draw round when cutting out the circle of greaseproof paper.

Cheese Flan and Mini Cheese Flans with Bacon

Proceed as before but also fry **2 or 3 rashers of lean bacon**, cut into small squares or matchsticks: add a little oil to the pan if necessary. The bacon should be cooked through but not crisp. Drain on kitchen paper and scatter over the bases of the pastry cases before you pour in the filling. Continue as before.

All-Butter Shortcrust Pastry

This is a richer version of the Plain Shortcrust Pastry.

160g (6oz) plain flour

80g (3oz) cold butter, diced

Pinch of salt

2 tbsp cold water

1. Tip the flour into the bowl of your food processor and add the butter and salt.

2. Whizz into fine crumbs.

3. Add the water and whizz again.

4. Once the mixture is starting to form big crumbs and clump together, turn it out onto a lightly floured board and knead it gently into a ball.

5. The pastry is now ready to use.

Savoury Summer Tartlets

The **All-Butter Shortcrust Pastry** above is ideal for a more elegant version of the cheese flans using 8 fluted tartlet tins.

Make the **All-Butter Shortcrust Pastry** as before and the filling from the **Mini Cheese Flans** recipe. You may like to leave out the onion.

Makes 8

Extra ingredients

A selection of fresh vegetables and herbs, such as:

Asparagus – thin spears or fatter ones sliced vertically

A few fresh peas or small mangetouts

Baby spinach leaves, torn slightly

Small florets of broccoli

Thinly sliced bell pepper

Baby sweetcorn – whole or sliced in half vertically – or sweetcorn kernels

Light scattering of 'soft' herbs such as: chives, chervil, dill, basil, or French tarragon

You will need 8 greased fluted loose-bottomed 10cm (4in) tartlet tins and a baking tray, plus baking beans (preferably ceramic) and greaseproof paper

1. Preheat the oven to 180°C (fan oven) or equivalent.

2. Cut out 8 circles of greaseproof paper using one of the loose bottoms as a template.

3. Divide the pastry into 8 equal pieces, roll out each one separately and line the tins.

4. Arrange the tins on the baking tray.

5. Put a circle of greaseproof paper in each one and fill almost to the brim with baking beans.

6. Bake for 12–15 minutes or until crisp and golden.

7. Leave to settle and cool in the tin.

8. Once cool, remove the baking beans from the pastry cases. Peel away the greaseproof paper circles.

9. Reduce the oven temperature to 160°C (fan ovens) or equivalent.

10. Add the filling and your choice of vegetables and herbs: some are better arranged on top of the filling, others are better laid in the cases before the filling is poured in.

11. Bake for approximately 15 minutes until risen and golden.

Using the pastry trimmings
Reroll the trimmings and use to make some jam tarts. The rerolled pastry is fine for small tarts but a little bit overworked for anything larger.

Walnut Pastry

The walnuts add a rich, nutty flavour and crumbliness to the pastry that works beautifully with creamy quiche-type fillings.

25g (1oz) walnuts, broken into pieces

25g (1oz) wholemeal flour

110g (4oz) plain flour

80g (3oz) cold butter, diced

Pinch of salt

1 tbsp cold water

1. Whizz the walnuts in the processor with the wholemeal flour until fine.

2. Add the plain flour, butter and salt.

3. Whizz into fine crumbs.

4. Add the water and whizz again.

5. Once the mixture is starting to form big crumbs and clump together, turn it out onto a lightly floured board and knead it gently into a ball.

6. The pastry is now ready to use.

Leek and Red Onion Tart with Walnut Pastry

Choose a crumbly white cheese such as Caerphilly, Wensleydale, Lancashire or White Cheshire to complement the beautiful flavours and textures of this unusual savoury tart.

Serves 4

Walnut Pastry

½ medium red onion, peeled

2 medium leeks, prepared

1 egg

1 egg yolk (keep white for sealing pastry case)

5 tbsp double cream

½ tsp made English mustard

50g (2oz) crumbly white cheese (see above, and Tip, below), grated

You will need a greased 18cm (7in) tart tin, a circle of greaseproof paper cut to fit, and baking beans

1. Preheat the oven to 180°C (fan oven) or equivalent.

2. Roll the pastry into a circle slightly larger than the tin.

3. Roll the pastry round the rolling pin and transfer to the tin.

4. Ease into shape; leave some pastry overhang and mould it gently into place. If tears occur, repair with offcuts.

5. Prick the base, fit the greaseproof paper circle in place and pour in the baking beans. Bake for around 15 minutes until golden.

6. Remove the greaseproof paper and baking beans. Brush the pastry with beaten egg white and return to the oven for 2–3 minutes.

7. Trim the overhang with a sharp knife, cutting outwards, away from the tin.

8. While the pastry case is baking, slice the onion and separate into crescents.

9. Cut the leeks into 2– 3cm (¾–1¼in) slices and steam until just tender; add the onions for a couple of minutes at the end. Drain on kitchen paper.

10. Whisk the egg, egg yolk, cream and mustard together until frothing and foamy.

11. Arrange the leeks in the pastry case with the onions and pour in the mixture. Scatter with cheese.

12. Bake for 15–20 minutes until puffed and golden. Serve warm or cold.

Tip
- You may also like to try making the tart with blue cheese for a change: Dolcelatte works well or a mellow, but not yet aggressive, Stilton.

Jam and Lemon Curd Tarts

These are the classic jam tarts that everyone enjoys. They are ideal to make with children but please observe the hot jam warnings.

Makes about 18

Plain Shortcrust or All-Butter Shortcrust Pastry

Raspberry, strawberry, apricot or blackcurrant jam, or lemon curd

You will need a 7.5cm (3in) fluted cutter and 2 greased 12-cup tart tins

1. Preheat the oven to 180°C (fan oven) or equivalent.

2. Roll the pastry gently with a lightly floured rolling pin on a floured board and cut into rounds. Press them gently into the tart tins.

3. Spoon in the jam (see Tip below).

4. Bake for 10–12 minutes until the pastry is lightly golden.

5. Allow time for the jam to cool then remove from the tin with a small palette knife and finish cooling on a wire rack.

Tip
- Fill each tart with no more than a slightly rounded teaspoon of jam or lemon curd: they need to be generously filled but not so much that as the jam or lemon curd heats up it boils out of the tarts.

Hot jam warnings
Keep the tart tins level as you take them out of the oven; if you tilt them at this stage the practically molten jam or curd will spill out of the tarts.

On no account eat the tarts while the jam is still runny. You will have the roof of your mouth off!

Deep Mini Jam and Lemon Curd Tartlets

Instead of using a standard tart tin for these, bake them in a mini-muffin tin: the result will be dinky little extra-deep jam tarts that could have come straight from a high-class patisserie window. If you prefer, you can make these with Sweet All-Butter Shortcrust (see page 112).

Makes approximately 24

Plain Shortcrust, All-Butter
   Shortcrust or Sweet All-Butter
   Shortcrust Pastry

Raspberry, strawberry, apricot or
   blackcurrant jam, or lemon curd

1. You will need a 6cm (2½in) fluted cutter and 2 greased 12-cup mini-muffin tins

2. Preheat the oven to 180°C (fan oven) or equivalent.

3. Turn the pastry out onto a lightly floured board and knead it lightly until it forms a ball.

4. Roll the pastry gently with a lightly floured rolling pin on a floured board and cut into rounds. Press them gently into the tart tins.

5. Spoon in the jam (see **Tip** for previous recipe).

6. Bake for 10–15 minutes until the pastry is lightly golden.

7. Allow time for the jam to cool then remove from the tin with a small palette knife and finish cooling on a wire rack.

Individual Treacle Tarts

These yummy little tarts have their sweetness balanced with lemon juice and work well made with unsweetened pastry such as Plain Shortcrust.

Makes about 18

Plain Shortcrust Pastry

4 tbsp golden syrup

40g (1½oz) soft dark brown sugar

Juice of 1 lemon, sieved

1 tsp vanilla extract

Pinch of salt

110g (4oz) breadcrumbs (see Tip)

1. You will need a 7.5cm (3in) fluted cutter and 2 greased 12-cup tart tins

2. Preheat the oven to 180°C (fan oven) or equivalent.

3. Warm the golden syrup and brown sugar over a moderate heat until of pouring consistency.

4. Remove from the heat and stir in the lemon juice, vanilla and salt.

5. Stir in the breadcrumbs, a few at a time, making sure they are all coated with syrup.

6. Roll the pastry gently with a lightly floured rolling pin on a floured board and cut into rounds. Press them gently into the tart tins.

7. Spoon the mixture into the pastry cases and smooth into position with the back of a wet teaspoon.

8. Bake for 12–15 minutes until the pastry is pale golden.

9. Cool slightly in the tin then transfer to a wire rack with a small palette knife to finish cooling.

Tip

- To make the breadcrumbs: remove the crusts from 110g (4oz) white or light wholemeal bread, tear into pieces and whizz briefly in the food processor until fine.

Sweet All-Butter Shortcrust Pastry

Use this recipe for sweet pastry recipes where the filling isn't too sweet. As well as sweetness, the sugar adds an extra crumbly quality..

160g (6oz) plain flour

80g (3oz) butter, cold and cut into small pieces

Pinch of salt

25g (1oz) caster sugar

2 tbsp cold water

1. Tip the flour into the bowl of your food processor and add the butter and salt.

2. Whizz into fine crumbs.

3. Add the sugar and whizz briefly

4. Add the water and whizz again.

5. Once the mixture is starting to form big crumbs and clump together, turn it out onto a lightly floured board and knead it gently into a ball.

6. The pastry is now ready to use.

Simple Raspberry Tarts

The Sweet All-Butter Shortcrust Pastry is the perfect partner for fragrant sweetly sharp raspberries in these easy tarts. There is no further baking involved once the pastry shells have been baked blind.

Makes 8

Sweet All-Butter Shortcrust Pastry

Raspberry jam or redcurrant jelly for spreading

1–2 punnets fresh raspberries

1 tsp icing sugar to finish

You will need 8 greased fluted loose-bottomed 10cm (4in) tartlet tins, and a baking tray, plus baking beans and greaseproof paper

1. Preheat the oven to 180°C (fan oven) or equivalent.

2. Cut out 8 circles of greaseproof paper using one of the loose bottoms as a template.

3. Divide the pastry into 8 equal pieces, roll out each one separately and line the tins.

4. Arrange the tins on the baking tray.

5. Put a circle of greaseproof paper in each one and fill almost to the brim with baking beans.

6. Bake for 12–15 minutes or until crisp and golden.

7. Leave to settle and cool in the tin.

8. Once cool, remove the baking beans from the pastry cases. Peel away the greaseproof paper circles.

9. Spread a little jam into the base of each pastry case with the back of a teaspoon.

10. Set the raspberries on top.

11. Just before serving, sift a little icing sugar over the top of each tart, stirring it through a tea strainer with a teaspoon.

Tip
- The pastry cases will store in an airtight tin for up to a week.

Simple Strawberry Tarts

The Sweet All-Butter Shortcrust also works beautifully as a foil for strawberries. Proceed as before but instead of raspberries lay **halved strawberries**, cut side down, over a layer of **sieved strawberry jam or redcurrant jelly**. Just before serving, sift a little icing sugar over the top of each tart, stirring it through a tea strainer with a teaspoon, or leave plain.

Other Simple Fruit Tarts

Use your imagination to create other simple fruit tarts: match your chosen fruit with a suitable jam or jelly. Tinned fruit in juice is always a good standby: apricot halves partnered with sieved apricot jam, for example, works particularly well.

Bakewell Tarts

You can use Plain Shortcrust or All-Butter Shortcrust for this recipe, or you may prefer to use the Sweet All-Butter Shortcrust. The Bakewell topping is also known as 'frangipane'.

Makes 15–16

Plain, All-Butter or Sweet All-Butter Shortcrust Pastry

75g (3oz) butter, softened

75g (3oz) caster sugar

40g (1½oz) plain flour

1 medium egg, beaten

½ tsp almond extract

110g (4oz) ground almonds

2 tbsp milk

Plus about 3 tbsp raspberry jam, preferably seedless

You will need 1 or 2 greased 12-cup tart tins and a 7.5cm (3in) cutter, fluted or plain

1. Preheat the oven to 180°C (fan oven) or equivalent.

2. Roll the pastry gently with a lightly floured rolling pin on a floured board and cut into rounds. Press them gently into the tart tins.

3. Whizz the butter and sugar together until light and fluffy.

4. Sieve in the flour and add the egg and almond extract.

5. Whizz briefly and add the ground almonds and milk.

6. Whizz again until thoroughly mixed.

7. Spoon a little jam in the base of each tart and top with a teaspoonful of the filling.

8. Smooth it gently with the back of a wet teaspoon, especially round the edges so the jam won't bubble through.

9. Bake for about 15–18 minutes or until the topping is risen and just tinged golden and the pastry is cooked.

10. Leave to settle for a few moments then ease from the tin with a small palette knife and cool on a wire rack.

11. Eat warm or cold.

12. Store in an airtight container when cold.

Almond Tarts

Make the Bakewell Tarts as in the previous recipe but instead of leaving them plain, scatter **flaked almonds** over the top of the tarts and press down lightly before they go into the oven. They look beautiful and taste delicious with a nicely contrasting crunch.

Coconut Tarts

These are made in exactly the same way as the Bakewell Tarts and Almond Tarts but with desiccated coconut rather than the ground almonds and almond extract.

Makes about 16

Plain, All-Butter or Sweet All-Butter Shortcrust Pastry

75g (3oz) butter, softened

75g (3oz) sugar

40g (1½oz) plain flour

1 egg, beaten

110g (4oz) desiccated coconut

2 tbsp milk

Plus about 3 tbsp raspberry jam, preferably seedless

You will need 1 or 2 greased 12-cup tart tins and a 7.5cm (3in) cutter, fluted or plain

1. Preheat the oven to 180°C (fan ovens) or equivalent.

2. Roll the pastry gently with a lightly floured rolling pin on a floured board and cut into rounds. Press them gently into the tart tins.

3. Whizz the butter and sugar together until light and fluffy.

4. Sieve in the flour and add the egg.

5. Whizz briefly and add the desiccated coconut and milk.

6. Whizz again until thoroughly mixed.

7. Spoon a little jam in the base of each tart and top with a teaspoonful of the filling.

8. Smooth it gently with the back of a wet teaspoon, especially round the edges so the jam won't bubble through.

9. Bake for about 15–18 minutes or until the coconut topping is risen and just tinged golden and the pastry is cooked.

10. Leave to settle for a few moments then ease from the tin with a small palette knife and cool on a wire rack.

11. Eat warm (but not hot) or cold.

12. Store in an airtight container when cold.

Apple Crumble Tarts

These are nice to make for a weekend tea: a winning combination of little apple tarts and well-loved apple crumble. The extra short, sweetened pastry really does make a difference: they are not quite as special made with ordinary shortcrust.

You really only need 12 teaspoons of crumble for this recipe: this equates to a little less than a quarter of a 225g (8oz) mix. Instructions have been given for the full amount, as it is very difficult to mix the very small amount needed successfully. This way, you have enough to make a crumble for lunchtime and the tarts for tea. Alternatively, you could freeze all but 12 spoonfuls of crumble for another day. You can freeze crumble for a short time, but don't leave it in the freezer for weeks and months as it starts to taste a bit stale and 'airy'.

You could make half the amount of crumble if you prefer, as you can make 110g (4oz) successfully, and freeze the rest.

Makes 12

Sweet All-Butter Shortcrust Pastry

For the crumble (see above for note on quantity)

225g (8oz) plain flour

1 level tsp baking powder

75g (3oz) butter, softened

75g (3oz) granulated sugar

For the filling

225g (8oz) eating apples (3 or 4 Cox's are ideal)

1–2 tbsp apple juice (or water)

1. You will need a greased 12-cup tart tin and a 7.5cm (3in) fluted cutter.

2. Preheat the oven to 180°C (fan oven) or equivalent.

3. Roll the pastry out gently with a floured rolling pin to a thickness of just less than half a centimetre.

4. Cut out 12 circles with the cutter. Transfer them to the prepared tart tin and firm them down gently.

5. To make the crumble: sieve the flour and baking powder into the bowl of your food processor. Whiz briefly and add the butter. Whiz again until the mixture forms fine crumbs. Add the sugar and whiz again very briefly.

Apple Crumble Tarts cont.

6. Peel and core the apples. Cut each apple in half and lay face down on your chopping surface. Cut length ways into half moon slices about a centimetre thick. Cook them gently for a few moments in a splash of apple juice or water until the juices are starting to run and they are softening slightly. Strain off any surplus juice and set aside.

7. Lay the apple slices in the base of each tart so that the base is covered. Top each tart with a spoonful of crumble mixture.

8. Bake for about 15 minutes or until the crumble is just tinged golden and the pastry is cooked. Ease from the tin with a small palette knife and cool on a wire rack. Eat warm or cold.

Classic Custard Tarts

Here is the classic custard tart: delicate, sweet and quivery egg custard in a crisp pastry case. This recipe involves first baking the pastry cases blind, which makes sure they are crisp with no trace of sogginess. Also, the custard filling can then be baked at a much lower temperature, which ensures it won't be bouncy or rubbery.

Another plus is tarts that won't 'weep' clear liquid: something that can happen if the delicate egg custard is cooked at too high a temperature or for too long.

You will need a 10cm (4in) pastry cutter and a 12-cup muffin tin. This is essential to get a good depth of custard. If you don't have a 10cm cutter, a 10cm fluted, individual flan tin or a 10cm plain, round food ring both make excellent alternatives. If you are using a fluted cutter, remove any excess pastry from around it whilst it is still pressed down on the board: if you try to remove it once you pick up the pastry you've cut out, you will stretch it out of shape.

Eat these fairly swiftly as the custard won't keep for more than a couple of days.

Makes 10

Sweet All-Butter Shortcrust Pastry

For the custard filling

1 egg

1 egg yolk

½ tsp vanilla extract

10g (½oz) caster sugar

4 tbsp double cream

Enough milk to make up the quantity to 300ml

Whole nutmeg, for grating

You will need a 12-cup muffin tin with 10 cups greased and a 10cm (4in) fluted or round cutter. Plus baking beans (preferably ceramic) and greaseproof paper, cut into 10 circles to fit the cups.

1. Preheat the oven to 180°C (fan oven) or equivalent.

2. Roll the pastry out gently on a very lightly floured board with a lightly floured rolling pin to a thickness of just less than half a centimetre.

3. Cut out the pastry rounds and using the tips of your first two fingers of each hand press them gently into the prepared muffin tin. Put a little circle of greaseproof paper in each one and fill almost to the brim with baking beans.

4. Bake for 15 minutes or until crisp and golden.

5. Leave to settle and cool slightly in the tin.

6. Reduce the oven temperature to 160°C (fan oven) or equivalent.

7. To make the custard filling, whisk the egg and egg yolk and pass through a sieve. A coiled bedspring-type whisk works well. Add the vanilla extract and sugar and whisk in. Whisk in the cream and the milk.

8. To assemble the tarts remove the baking beans from the pastry cases. Peel away the greaseproof paper circles.

9. Pour the filling into the cases and grate nutmeg over the top. Be careful not to fill them too full and try to avoid spilling any between the pastry cases and the tin.

Classic Custard Tarts cont.

10. Bake for 12 minutes or until the custard is rising slightly and developing a very light skin. *Don't overcook!*

11. Leave to rest and cool in the tin for a while and then remove carefully, easing them out with a small palette knife. Transfer to a wire rack to finish cooling.

A Note on Grating Nutmeg

When you are grating nutmeg, make sure you grate some of the outside each time. If you just grate the inside part, once it is exposed, you won't get quite such a characteristic speckled effect – it will be more of a uniform pale brown powder.

Extra Rich Sweet All-Butter Shortcrust Pastry

This recipe is for a sweet all-butter shortcrust pastry, with a bit more butter and a bit less water than usual. The result is a gloriously short and rich pastry, very like shortbread in fact: it's absolutely perfect for mince pies.

180g (6oz) plain flour

120g (4oz) cold butter

Pinch of salt

25g (1oz) caster sugar

1 tbsp cold water

1. Tip the flour into the bowl of your food processor and add the butter and salt.

2. Whizz into fine crumbs.

3. Add the sugar and whizz briefly.

4. Add the water and whizz again.

5. Once the mixture is starting to form big crumbs and clump together, turn it out onto a lightly floured board and knead it gently into a ball.

6. The pastry is now ready to use.

Mince Pies with Extra Rich Sweet All-Butter Pastry

When you are making your own mince pies, it's important that both components are equally good: short and delicious pastry and fresh and fruity mincemeat, with maybe just a little hint of brandy.

If you have made your own mincemeat (see recipe for Butter Mincemeat on page 122) then your pies should be really special.

Makes 12

Extra Rich Sweet All-Butter Shortcrust Pastry

Approximately 12 tsp mincemeat

Caster sugar for finishing

You will need 1 x 7.5cm (3in) and 1 x 6cm (2½in) fluted cutter and a greased 12-cup tart tin

1. Preheat the oven to 180°C (fan oven) or equivalent.

2. Roll the pastry gently with a lightly floured rolling pin on a floured board.

3. Cut out 12 rounds with the larger cutter and 12 rounds with the smaller cutter.

4. Press the larger rounds gently into the tart tin.

5. Put about a teaspoon of mincemeat into each: don't overfill as the mincemeat can boil out.

6. Brush the edge of each lid with water and pat them very gently onto the pies with your fingertips.

7. Brush each pie with water and sprinkle a little caster sugar over the top.

8. Make a little hole in each lid with the point of a knife.

9. Bake for about 12 minutes or until pale golden.

10. Remove from the tin and cool on a wire rack.

Tip
- The pastry is very short and rich so to avoid breaking the pies when removing them from the tin, bear the following points in mind:

- Ideally, your tart tin should be non-stick and in perfect condition.

- Avoid pressing the lids down too hard and squashing the pastry over the top of the tin.

- Leave the pies to cool down slightly before attempting to remove them with the aid of a small short-handled palette knife.

Butter Mincemeat

Apart from using the grating side of the grating/slicing blade to grate the apples, you won't need your food processor for this recipe. However, it complements the Extra Rich All-Butter Pastry perfectly, lifting your mince pies to another level, so is included here.

This is a slight variation on traditional mincemeat in that it uses butter rather than shredded suet as the fat component. You need some form of fat in your mincemeat to give the characteristic smoothness and lusciousness to the flavour and texture. The traditional suet is a remnant of the centuries old original recipes for mincemeat, which were savoury and contained actual minced meat.

This butter version is a handy alternative for vegetarians – although not for vegans.

Makes approximately 1.5kg (a little over 3lb)

175g (6oz) butter, diced: salted or unsalted are both suitable

Finely grated zest and juice of 1 orange

Finely grated zest and juice of 1 lemon

225g (8oz) firm dessert apples, peeled and cored (prepared weight)

225g (8oz) raisins

225g (8oz) sultanas

225g (8oz) currants

225g (8oz) soft dark brown sugar

110g (4oz) candied peel, cut into fine pieces

2-3 tsp mixed spice

150ml (¼pt) brandy

You will need a large bowl or preferably a lidded casserole dish

1. Melt the butter over a low heat.

2. Strain the orange and lemon juice through a sieve and zest the peel into short pieces.

3. Grate the apples.

4. Put into the bowl with all the other ingredients, mix thoroughly and stir in the melted butter.

5. Leave overnight in a cool place for the flavours to amalgamate.

6. Next day give everything a stir and spoon into sterilised jars. Try to avoid leaving any air pockets: keep turning the jars round to check and push the mincemeat down with a dinner knife if you see any.

Tips
- Always use firm dessert apples for your mincemeat and never use windfalls – they may have already started to ferment and would continue to ferment in the jars.

- The lemon and orange zest won't be cooked or processed further so be sure to zest in brisk up-and-down movements to avoid long strands in the finished mincemeat: you may also like to run a sharp knife over the zest on a board as extra insurance.

Sterilising jars
Wash the jars in hot soapy water and rinse thoroughly. Shake off any excess water and stand on a baking tray. Put into the oven for 10 minutes or so at 160°C or equivalent. Alternatively, you can put them through the hottest cycle of your dishwasher if you have one.

Christmas Spiced Mini Apple Pies

These are a useful and delicious alternative to offer with mince pies at Christmas.

Makes 12

Extra Rich Sweet All-Butter
  Shortcrust Pastry

10g (½oz) butter

1 rounded tsp soft brown sugar

¼ tsp mixed spice

¼ tsp powdered ginger

¼ tsp powdered cinnamon

2-3 dessert apples, peeled and
  cored, approximately 200g (7oz)
  prepared weight

40g (1½oz) sultanas (optional)

You will need 1 x 7.5cm (3in) and
1 x 6cm (2½in) fluted cutter and a
greased 12-cup tart tin

1. Preheat the oven to 180°C (fan oven) or equivalent.

2. Roll the pastry gently with a lightly floured rolling pin on a floured board.

3. Cut out 12 rounds with the larger cutter and 12 rounds with the smaller cutter.

4. Press the larger rounds gently into the tart tin.

5. Melt the butter and sugar together over a gentle heat, add the spices.

6. Cut the apple into small pieces and stir into the melted butter mixture making sure each piece is coated.

7. Add the sultanas, stir into the mixture in the same way.

8. Cook gently, stirring the mixture carefully round the pan, until the apple is just starting to soften and the sultanas are plumping up.

9. Divide the apple filling equally among the pastry cases.

10. Brush the edge of each lid with water and pat them very gently onto the pies with your fingertips.

11. Brush each pie with water and sprinkle a little caster sugar over the top.

12. Make a little hole in each lid with the point of a knife.

13. Bake for about 12 minutes or until pale golden. Remove from the tin and cool on a wire rack.

Tip
- Don't stir the apple mixture too vigorously as the small apple pieces need to stay whole in the finished pies.

Mini Picnic Apple Pies

You can make a plainer version of the Christmas Apple Pies at any time of year: they are handy for lunch boxes and picnics. Proceed as before but leave out the spices and sultanas, although you may like to add a pinch of cinnamon.

Pasty Pastry

In complete contrast to the rich crumbliness of the previous pastry, here is a shortcrust pastry that will stand you in good stead for pasties and fruit pies.

This pastry is made using strong bread flour and it works brilliantly: it makes a slightly flaky and more elastic dough, delicious and handy for easing over the bumpy filling.

175g (6oz) strong white bread flour

40g (1½oz) cold butter, diced

40g (1½oz) lard or cold block vegetable shortening, diced

½ tsp salt

2 tbsp cold water

1. Tip the flour into the bowl of your food processor and add the butter, lard or vegetable shortening and salt.

2. Whizz into fine crumbs.

3. Add the water and whizz again.

4. Once the mixture is starting to form big crumbs and clump together, turn it out onto a lightly floured board and knead it gently into a ball.

5. The pastry is now ready to use.

Tip
- Use the pastry straight away, as it doesn't respond well to chilling, and be careful not to overwork it.

Steak Pasty Cornish Style

Strictly speaking, a Cornish pasty should be made by a Cornish person, in Cornwall. This recipe is very close to the genuine article. In the traditional manner, the meat and vegetables aren't precooked but cut into pieces small enough to cook within the pasty. No hole or vent is made for the steam to escape as the steam helps to cook the filling in a kind of 'mini steam oven'.

Makes 2 average-size pasties or 3 smaller ones

Pasty Pastry

1 smallish onion

1 smallish potato

A piece of swede slightly smaller than the potato

110g (4oz) chuck or blade or skirt steak

Plenty of freshly ground black pepper and a touch of salt

1 egg beaten with 1 tsp water to glaze

You will need a greased baking tray

1. Preheat the oven to 180°C (fan oven) or equivalent.

2. Peel and slice the vegetables to a thickness of 1–2mm.

3. Cut them crossways into pieces not much larger than 1cm. Slice the steak in the same way.

4. Roll out the pastry and cut into circles using a plate or cereal bowl to guide you.

5. Lay the circles onto the greased baking tray.

6. Put your filling in the middle of each, seasoning with plenty of pepper and a little salt as you go.

7. Brush the edges of the pastry with water.

8. Gather the pastry from the sides and bring them together at the top, gently pressing them together as you go. This will give you the characteristic wavy 'crimp'.

9. Brush with beaten egg for a glossy professional finish and bake for 20–25 minutes or until golden brown.

10. Eat hot or cold.

Tip
- Pasties can be 'crimped' at the top or the side. You may find the 'top crimp' easier to manage.

Caution
If you are going to eat your pasty hot, cut into it first and wait a few moments for the steam to escape, otherwise you could give yourself a nasty pasty burn.

Cheese and Onion Pasty

These are equally as delicious as the steak version.

Makes 2 average-size pasties or 3 smaller ones

Pasty Pastry

1 small onion

1 smallish potato

25–50g (1–2oz) Cheddar cheese

Plenty of freshly ground black pepper

You will need a greased baking tray

1. Preheat the oven to 180°C (fan oven) or equivalent.

2. Proceed as above. The potato and onion should be sliced thinly, as before.

3. Dice the cheese into roughly 1cm cubes: this is the optimum size to allow it to melt but not dry out and frazzle.

4. Continue as before.

Savoury Tartlets Elodie with Smoked Salmon, Bacon and Mango Chutney

The extreme savouriness of the smoked salmon and bacon are complemented by the mango chutney – sweet with just a hint of mellow spiciness. The ricotta blends beautifully with the egg and semi-skimmed milk to make a wonderfully light savoury custard.

Makes 8 tarts: serves 8 as a starter, 4 as a main course

All-Butter Shortcrust Pastry

Filling

2-3 rashers lean back bacon, snipped into small pieces

A little oil for frying

2 tsp mango chutney: any large pieces of mango cut small

50-60g (2-2?oz) smoked salmon

100g (4oz) ricotta, drained of whey

1 egg

1 egg yolk (keep white for sealing pastry case)

Freshly ground black pepper

1 tbsp semi-skimmed milk

You will need 8 x greased fluted, loose bottomed, 10cm tartlet tins, a baking tray, plus baking beans and greaseproof paper

To serve

Leafy green salad

1. Preheat the oven to 180C (fan oven) or equivalent

2. Cut out 8 circles of greaseproof paper using one of the loose bottoms as a template.

3. Divide the pastry into 8 equal pieces, roll out each one into a circle and line the tins leaving some pastry overhang.

4. Arrange the tins on the baking tray. Prick the base, fit the greaseproof paper circle in place and pour in the baking beans.

5. Bake for around 10-12 minutes until golden. Brush with beaten egg white and return to the oven for 2-3 minutes.

6. Trim the overhang with a sharp knife cutting outwards, away from the tin. Once cool, remove the baking beans from the pastry cases. Peel away the greaseproof paper circles and set aside.

7. Fry the bacon until cooked through but not crisp. Drain on kitchen paper and set aside.

8. Pound the ricotta until smooth. Stir in the milk.

9. Whisk the egg, egg yolk and pepper together. Combine with the ricotta and milk and set aside.

10. Dab the mango chutney over the base of each pastry case and scatter the bacon over. Snip the salmon over the top using kitchen scissors.

11. Pour in the savoury custard. Bake for 15-20 minutes until puffed and golden. Serve warm or cold.

Steak and Potato Pie

This is a great heartening pie for a winter weekend lunch or supper. You will need one of those old-fashioned pie funnels to stop the pastry from falling into the filling.

Serves 4

Pasty Pastry

For the filling

450g (1lb) potatoes

450g (1lb) braising steak,

or preferably feather steak (ask your local butcher)

1 tbsp plain flour

Oil for frying

1 fair-sized onion

1 tbsp Worcestershire sauce

1 tsp black treacle

Freshly ground black or white pepper

¼ tsp salt, or to taste

Beaten egg to glaze

You will need a 1¼ litre (2 pint) pie dish with a flat rim, and a pie funnel

To make the filling

1. Peel the potatoes, cut into quarters and boil in unsalted water until just tender. Drain and set aside to cool, but keep the cooking water.

2. Cut the steak into bite-sized pieces, and coat in the flour. Heat the oil in a pan and fry the onion. Remove from the pan and keep warm, check there is enough oil left in the pan and fry the meat, turning frequently until it is lightly browned. Return the onion to the pan. Put the Worcestershire sauce and black treacle into about 275ml (½ pint) of the cooking water from the potatoes, and add to the pan, season with pepper.

3. Stir it all together and bring to the boil, stirring frequently. Leave it to simmer gently, stirring from time to time, until the meat is tender and the gravy has thickened. Top up with more potato water if necessary. Check for seasoning and add any salt towards the end. Meanwhile, make the pastry.

Steak and Potato Pie cont.

To make the pie

1. Flour your rolling pin and work surface and roll the dough to a thickness of slightly less than 1/2cm. Put your pie dish upside down onto the pastry and cut round it so you have a piece of pastry slightly larger than your dish.

2. Grease the rim of the dish. Using the leftover pastry, cut some strips the right width and press gently all round the rim. Use your rolling pin to firm it gently. Put the filling into the dish with enough gravy to cover. Reserve the rest of the gravy. Put your pie funnel into the centre of the pie filling. Slice your cooked potatoes and arrange in a thick layer over the top.

3. Brush the pastry rim with water. Lift your pastry lid into position on the pie. Ease the pastry down over the funnel so it shows through. Press the edges down gently. Finally, brush the top with beaten egg and bake in a preheated oven at 180°C (fan oven) or equivalent for about 20 minutes or until the pastry is golden brown.

4. Serve with the leftover gravy heated until piping hot and steamed vegetables.

Old-Fashioned Apple Plate Pie

The Pasty Pastry is ideal for this old-fashioned plate pie, also known as a 'one-crust' pie, which means it has a pastry lid, but no bottom. The Pasty Pastry fits easily over the bumpy apple filling without tearing.

Pasty Pastry

3 dessert apples: Cox's are perfect

1 tbsp apple juice (or water if no juice available)

Caster sugar for finishing

You will need a greased 23cm (9in) pie plate

1. Preheat the oven to 180°C (fan oven) or equivalent.

2. Roll the pastry gently with a lightly floured rolling pin on a floured board.

3. Put your pie plate on top of the rolled out pastry and cut round it with a knife so that you end up with a circle slightly larger than the plate.

4. Peel and core the apples and slice them thinly.

5. Arrange them evenly in the pie plate, piling them up slightly in the middle.

6. Add the apple juice or water.

7. Grease the rim of the plate and cut some strips from the leftover pastry the width of the rim.

8. Use some of these strips to line the rim: press them down gently so that they join together.

9. Brush the pastry rim with water and lift your circle of pastry on top: you might like to use your rolling pin to lift it.

10. Brush the top of the pie with water and sprinkle with caster sugar. Make a neat slit in the top with your knife.

11. Bake for 20–25 minutes, or until the pie is pale golden brown on top.

Old-Fashioned Rhubarb Plate Pie

This is a version of the apple pie above, made with rhubarb. Rhubarb makes such a lot of juice that it's better to part cook it without sugar first so you can drain most of it away. If you don't, juice will bubble and run everywhere and seep into the pastry, making it soggy.

Pasty Pastry

About 700g (1½lb) rhubarb

75–110g (3–4oz) granulated sugar

Caster sugar for finishing

1. Preheat the oven to 180°C (fan oven) or equivalent.

2. Trim the rhubarb and cut into short lengths.

3. Put into a saucepan with 1–2 tablespoons of water and cook gently until it is starting to soften and the juices are running.

4. Remove from the heat, strain off the juice and discard.

5. Roll out your pastry as above and arrange the strained rhubarb in a pie plate.

6. Sprinkle the granulated sugar over it and stir it in lightly.

7. Continue as before.

Rich Chocolate Shortcrust Pastry

As mentioned in Chapter 9, 'Biscuits', sweet shortcrust pastry and some biscuit doughs have a lot in common. This beautiful deep chocolate-flavoured pastry is practically identical to the Chocolate Biscuits recipe on page 142.

160g (5oz) plain flour

20g (1oz) cocoa powder

60g (3oz) cold butter, diced

50g (2oz) caster sugar

3 tablespoons cold milk

1. Tip the flour and cocoa into the bowl of your food processor and add the butter.

2. Whizz into fine crumbs.

3. Add the sugar and whizz briefly.

4. Add the milk and whizz again.

5. Once the mixture is starting to form big crumbs and clump together, turn it out onto a lightly floured board (it will be quite crumbly still) and knead it gently into a ball.

5. The pastry is now ready to use.

Quick and Easy Chocolate and Cherry Tarts

These delicious and deceptively impressive tarts are based on the flavours of that old retro favourite black forest gateau. Assemble just before serving for best results.

You can make the chocolate pastry cases ahead of time and store in an airtight tin until needed. You may also like to whip the cream before the meal and leave it in the fridge.

Makes 6

6 x pastry cases made with Rich Chocolate Shortcrust Pastry as before plus:

600g (1lb 5oz) jar of cherry compote

300ml (10 fl oz) double cream

Chocolate sprinkles or grated chocolate to serve

1. Divide the compote between the pastry cases.

2. Whip the cream to soft peaks.

3. Spoon (or pipe using a star nozzle) the cream on top of the compote and finish with the sprinkles or grated chocolate.

Tip

- For added luxury, you may like to add a tablespoon of sieved icing sugar to the cream before whipping and fold in a couple of tablespoons of brandy or kirsch before topping the tarts. If fresh cherries are available, a few would make a welcome extra garnish.

Chocolate Tarts with Chocolate Pastry

These gorgeous chocolate tarts are no trouble to make. Once the pastry cases are baked, there is no further cooking involved beyond melting the chocolate. Use all milk chocolate for a sweeter version if you prefer.

Makes 6

Rich Chocolate Shortcrust Pastry

50g (2 oz) good quality dark chocolate

50g (2 oz) good quality milk chocolate

15g (½oz) butter, softened

3 tbsp double cream

To serve

Fresh raspberries or strawberries and a dollop of clotted cream.

You will need 6 greased fluted loose-bottomed 10cm (4in) tartlet tins and a baking tray, plus baking beans and greaseproof paper

1. Preheat the oven to 180°C (fan oven) or equivalent.

2. Cut out 6 circles of greaseproof paper using one of the loose bottoms as a template.

3. Divide the pastry into 6 equal pieces, roll out each one separately and line the tins.

4. Arrange the tins on the baking tray.

5. Put a circle of greaseproof paper in each one and fill almost to the brim with baking beans.

6. Bake for 12–15 minutes or until crisp.

7. Leave to settle and cool in the tin.

8. Once cool, remove the baking beans from the pastry cases. Peel away the greaseproof paper circles.

9. Once the cases are ready to use, break up the chocolate and put it into a heatproof bowl. Melt the chocolate in the microwave on High, in 30-second bursts: it will take a couple of minutes or so in all.

10. (Alternatively, melt the chocolate in a bowl over a pan of barely simmering water: choose a bowl that will fit comfortably in the top of the saucepan but without the bottom touching the hot water.)

11. Cut the butter into small pieces and stir into the chocolate towards the end of the melting time.

12. Stir in the cream and divide the filling among the pastry cases.

13. Leave in a cool place to set.

14. Serve with fresh raspberries or strawberries and a dollop of clotted cream.

Chocolate Tarts with Chocolate Pastry cont.

Tips
- The pastry cases will store in an airtight tin for up to a week.

- Use any pastry trimmings from the tarts to make a few small biscuits. Bake for 7–8 minutes at 180°C (fan oven) or equivalent.

Mix and Match

You may like to experiment and mix and match some of the different pastries and fillings to suit yourself: for example, try making Chocolate Tarts with Sweet All-Butter Shortcrust Pastry, or Raspberry or Strawberry Tarts with Rich Chocolate Pastry.

Chapter 9

Biscuits

The kind of biscuit dough you roll and cut out (as opposed to the kind made by melting the ingredients together and spooning the mixture onto the baking tray) has much in common with sweet shortcrust pastry.

The ingredients for making this kind of biscuit or cookie dough in the food processor are similar to those for sweet shortcrust pastry: fat, flour and sugar are the basis, often with egg or milk to make the dough richer or more malleable.

The method is a kind of hybrid of cake and pastry making, often creaming the fat and flour together first.

- As with pastry, be careful not to overwork the dough or reroll too much or get too much flour on your board.

- Once you have made your biscuit mixture, the other two common pitfalls of biscuit making are rolling your dough too thinly and leaving the biscuits in the oven for too long.

- In most cases, roll the dough to a depth of a fraction less than the thickness of a pound coin.

- Be careful not to overcook biscuits as they can burn very easily: it only takes a minute to overdo them by mistake. Always use a timer so you know when to check.

- When biscuits first come out of the oven they are still soft and you might be tempted to put them back for a minute or two. Don't: they will soon harden as they cool down.

- Some biscuits are meant to be more of a slightly chewy cookie consistency rather than crisp and brittle.

- Get to know your oven and make notes of cooking times and temperatures that work for a particular recipe in your oven and refer back to them.

- If you don't want to make all your biscuits straight away, you can store the dough in the fridge for a few days or freeze it. Defrost frozen dough overnight in the fridge and take dough out of the fridge 20 minutes or so before you need to use it.

Use the normal blade attachment of your processor for all the recipes in this chapter.

Vanilla Biscuits

These light, crisp biscuits are very moreish indeed. They have a beautiful flavour – half a teaspoon of vanilla extract is exactly right, so don't be tempted to add a bit more 'for luck'. Don't forget, the biscuits will be very soft when they come out of the oven, but will harden as they cool.

Makes approximately 30 biscuits

150g (5oz) butter, softened

110g (4oz) caster sugar

1 egg, beaten

½ tsp vanilla extract

200g (7oz) plain flour

2 level tsp baking powder

You will need a large greased baking tray and a plain 6cm (2½in) cutter

1. Preheat the oven to 180°C (fan oven) or equivalent.

2. Whizz the butter and sugar together until light and fluffy.

3. Add the vanilla to the egg.

4. Add the baking powder to the weighed flour and sieve about half over the mixture, add the egg and vanilla and sieve the rest of the flour on top.

5. Whizz until the mixture starts to clump together, then stop the machine. You may have to do this in stages, as the mixture is quite dense, removing the lid and scraping the mixture down from the sides three or four times, particularly at the beginning.

6. Scoop the mixture out of the machine and knead it lightly together on a floured board. It's quite soft and delicate to work with, so keep everything lightly floured and treat it gently.

7. Roll the dough to a thickness of just less than a pound coin. Cut into rounds and transfer to the prepared baking sheet: use a palette knife to help you as the mixture is quite delicate.

8. Leave space between the biscuits as they spread during baking. Bake for 5–7 minutes until the biscuits are pale golden, but not at all brown.

9. Leave to cool and harden for a couple of minutes, no more, on the tray, and then transfer to a cooling rack, using a palette knife.

10. Once the biscuits are completely cold, store in an airtight tin.

Tip
- It is easier to manage the dough if you divide it into two pieces and make the biscuits in two batches.

Coconut Biscuits

These have a gorgeous, slightly crumbly quality and melt in the mouth. The recipe is very similar to the Vanilla Biscuits one but the addition of coconut makes a slightly firmer dough. A round fluted cutter works perfectly well but if you have a similar size square one it looks really effective.

Makes approximately 30 biscuits

150g (5oz) butter, softened

110g (4oz) caster sugar, plus extra for finishing (optional)

150g (5oz) plain flour

2 level tsp baking powder

1 medium egg, beaten

50g (2oz) desiccated coconut

You will need a large greased baking tray and a fluted 6cm (2½in) cutter

1. Preheat the oven to 180°C (fan oven) or equivalent.

2. Whizz the butter and sugar together until light and fluffy.

3. Add the baking powder to the weighed flour and sieve about half over the mixture, add the egg and sieve the rest of the flour on top.

4. Whizz to mix and add the coconut.

5. Whizz until the mixture starts to clump together, then stop the machine. You may have to do this in stages, as the mixture is quite dense, removing the lid and scraping the mixture down from the sides three or four times, particularly at the beginning.

6. Scoop the mixture out of the machine and knead it lightly together on a floured board. It's quite soft and delicate to work with, so keep everything lightly floured and treat it gently.

7. Roll the dough to a thickness of just less than a pound coin.

8. Cut into rounds and transfer to the prepared baking sheet: use a palette knife to help you as the mixture is quite delicate.

9. Bake for 5–7 minutes until the biscuits are pale golden, but not at all brown.

10. Leave to cool and harden for a couple of minutes, no more, on the tray, and then transfer to a cooling rack, using a palette knife: you may like to sprinkle the biscuits with caster sugar while they are still warm.

11. Once they are completely cold, store in an airtight tin.

Tip
- It is easier to manage the dough if you divide it into two pieces and make the biscuits in two batches.

Almond Biscuits

Again, this recipe is very similar to the one for Vanilla Biscuits but, as with the desiccated coconut in the Coconut version, the ground almonds make a firmer dough that doesn't spread as much during baking. This makes it possible to use a fluted cutter to cut out the rounds, which gives a nice professional look. Gorgeous with a cup of tea, these are also ideal to serve with ice cream and creamy or mousse-type puddings.

Makes approximately 34 biscuits

150g (5oz) butter, slightly softened

110g (4oz) caster sugar

150g (5oz) plain flour

2 level tsp baking powder

1 medium egg, beaten

½ tsp natural almond extract

50g (2oz) ground almonds

You will need a large greased baking tray and a fluted 6cm (2½in) cutter

1. Preheat the oven to 180°C (fan ovens) or equivalent.

2. Whizz the butter and sugar together until light and fluffy.

3. Add the baking powder to the weighed flour and sieve about half over the mixture, add the egg and almond extract and sieve the rest of the flour on top.

4. Whizz to mix and add the ground almonds.

5. Whizz until the mixture is starting to come together and then stop and scrape any mixture down from the sides.

6. Whizz until the mixture starts to clump together, then stop the machine. You may have to do this in stages, as the mixture is quite dense, removing the lid and scraping the mixture down from the sides three or four times, particularly at the beginning.

7. Scoop the mixture out of the machine and knead it lightly together on a floured board. It's quite soft and delicate to work with, so keep everything lightly floured and treat it gently.

8. Roll the dough to a thickness of just less than a pound coin.

9. Cut into rounds and transfer to the prepared baking tray: use a palette knife to help you as the mixture is quite delicate.

10. Bake for 5–7 minutes until the biscuits are pale golden, but not at all brown.

11. Leave to cool and harden for a couple of minutes, no more, on the tray, and then transfer to a cooling rack, using a palette knife: you may like to sprinkle the biscuits with caster sugar while they are still warm.

12. Once they are completely cold, store in an airtight tin.

Chocolate Biscuits

Simple to make and very child-friendly, these biscuits have a beautiful deep chocolatey taste. They lend themselves to all kinds of shaped cutters and are fun for children to make.

Makes up to 30 biscuits, depending on cutter size

110g (4oz) butter, softened

50g (2oz) caster sugar

160g (5½oz) plain flour

40g (1½oz) cocoa powder

2 tbsp semi-skimmed milk

You will need a large greased baking tray

1. Preheat the oven to 180°C (fan oven) or equivalent.

2. Whizz the butter and sugar together until fluffy.

3. Sieve in the flour and cocoa.

4. Whizz again.

5. Add the milk and whizz until the mixture comes together in large clumps.

6. Turn it out onto a lightly floured board and form it gently into a ball.

7. Roll out on the lightly floured board using a lightly floured rolling pin to the thickness of a little less than a pound coin.

8. Cut into rounds or other shapes with your chosen cutters and arrange on the greased baking tray.

9. Reroll the trimmings until you have used up all the dough.

10. Bake for approximately 7–8 minutes.

11. Almost immediately lift from the tray with a small palette knife and cool on a wire rack.

12. Once cold, store in an airtight container.

Tips
- Brush the biscuits with milk if they look a bit dusty and floury once they are on the tray.

- It is easier to manage the dough if you divide it into two pieces and make the biscuits in two batches.

Orange Biscuits

These are lovely and light and zesty, perfect with a cup of tea or coffee.

Makes approximately 30 biscuits

150g (5oz) butter, softened

110g (4oz) caster sugar

200g (7oz) plain flour

2 level tsp baking powder

1 medium egg, beaten

Finely grated zest of 2 oranges

You will need a large greased baking tray and a round 6cm (2½in) cutter

1. Preheat the oven to 180°C (fan ovens) or equivalent.

2. Whizz the butter and sugar together until fluffy.

3. Add the baking powder to the weighed flour and sieve about half the flour and baking powder over the mixture.

4. Add the egg and orange zest and the rest of the flour.

5. Whizz until the mixture starts to come together in large clumps.

6. You may have to stop the machine and scrape the mixture down from the sides a couple of times at the beginning as it is quite a stiff mixture.

7. Scoop the mixture out of the machine and knead it lightly together on a floured board.

8. Roll out to a thickness of just less than a pound coin.

9. Cut out rounds.

10. Transfer to the prepared baking sheet: use a palette knife to help you as the mixture is quite delicate: leave space between the biscuits as they spread during cooking.

11. Bake for 5–7 minutes until the biscuits are pale golden, but not at all brown.

12. Leave to cool for a couple of minutes, no more, on the tray, and then transfer to a cooling rack, using a palette knife. The biscuits are very soft when they come out of the oven, but will harden as they cool.

13. Once they are cold, store in an airtight container.

Tip
- It is easier to manage the dough if you divide it into two pieces and make the biscuits in two batches.

Lemon Biscuits

These are made in exactly the same way as the Orange Biscuits above, but use **the zest of 2 lemons** instead of oranges.

Shrewsbury-type Biscuits

This is a handy recipe: you can also use it for Easter Biscuits at Easter or as Christmas Cookies at Christmas. Cut out the dough with either a fluted round or suitably themed novelty cutter.

Makes approximately 24

110g (4oz) butter, softened

110g (4oz) caster sugar

200g (7oz) plain flour

¼ tsp mixed spice

1 whole egg and 1 egg yolk, beaten

You will need a large greased baking tray and a fluted 6cm (2½in) cutter

1. Preheat the oven to 180°C (fan oven) or equivalent.

2. Whizz the butter and sugar together until fluffy.

3. Sieve half the flour and spice over the mixture and add the egg and egg yolk.

4. Add the rest of the flour.

5. Whizz until the mixture starts to come together in large clumps.

6. You may have to stop the machine and scrape the mixture down from the sides a couple of times at the beginning as it is quite a stiff mixture.

7. Scoop the mixture out of the machine and knead it lightly together on a floured board.

8. Roll out on the lightly floured board using a lightly floured rolling pin to the thickness of just less than a pound coin.

9. Cut out rounds or other shapes with your chosen cutters.

10. Transfer to the prepared baking tray.

11. Bake for 5–7 minutes until the biscuits are pale golden, but not at all brown.

12. Sprinkle the biscuits with caster sugar while they are still warm and transfer to a wire rack to cool.

13. Once cooled, they will keep in an airtight tin for several days.

Tips
- If you prefer, instead of spice, flavour your biscuits with the **finely grated zest of a lemon** or **½ tsp of vanilla extract**.

- It is easier to manage the dough if you divide it into two pieces and make the biscuits in two batches.

Icing and Finishing Christmas Cookies

You can decorate the cookies in a variety of ways:

- Sprinkle with coloured sugar (look in the baking section of most stores) before they go into the oven.
- Press a chocolate button into the cookies when they come out of the oven and are still warm. This works with Smarties and mini Smarties too.
- Pipe with lines of glacé icing when completely cold: use Lemon Glacé Icing (page 00). Sprinkle with coloured sugar or press Smarties lightly into the icing.

Fruit Shrewsbury Biscuits

Proceed as before. Once the dough is mixed remove the processor blade and work in **110g (4oz) currants** and continue as before.

Malted Muesli Biscuits

These scrummy little biscuits are just the thing to keep you going if energy is flagging a little. They are also great for picnics and lunch boxes or to offer with a sociable cup of tea on a free afternoon. They don't contain much sugar as the malt extract is naturally sweet.

Makes about 22 biscuits

110g (4oz) butter, softened

50g (2oz) soft brown sugar

1 level tbsp barley malt extract

1 tbsp milk

110g (4oz) wholemeal flour

110g (4oz) unsweetened muesli (any large nuts should be chopped into smaller pieces)

You will need a greased baking tray.

1. Preheat the oven to 180°C (fan oven) or equivalent.

2. Whiz the butter and sugar together until combined and fluffy and add the malt extract. Whiz again to combine. Add the milk and wholemeal flour and whiz until thoroughly mixed.

3. Remove the blade from the machine and stir in the muesli, making sure it is evenly distributed throughout the mixture.

4. Take teaspoons of the mixture and roll into balls about the size of a walnut. Space these out evenly on the prepared baking tray. Use a fork to flatten each ball into a disc shape (you are not making fork biscuits as such: the biscuits will spread slightly during baking).

5. Bake for 7–8 minutes until they are just starting to go golden brown around the edges.

6. Leave to settle for a moment or two and then transfer to a wire cooling rack, using a small palette knife. They will still be soft at this stage but will firm up as they cool.

7. Once cool, store in an airtight container. Wrap them closely in foil inside the container to keep them extra fresh.

8. You can eat these warm if you like, once the outside has firmed but the middle is still soft.

Malted Ginger Oat Biscuits

There is something very yummy and appealing to the taste about anything malted. Here, a spoonful is added to these little oaty biscuits.

Makes about 22 biscuits

110g (4oz) butter, softened

50g (2oz) soft brown sugar

1 level tbsp barley malt extract

110g (4oz) wholemeal flour

Pinch salt

1-2 tsp ground ginger

1 tbsp milk

110g (4oz) porridge o

You will need a greased baking tray.

1. Preheat the oven to 180°C (fan oven) or equivalent.

2. Whiz the butter and sugar together until combined and fluffy and add the malt extract. Whiz again to combine. Add the wholemeal flour, salt, ginger and milk and whiz until thoroughly mixed.

3. Remove the blade from the machine and stir in the oats, a few at a time, making sure they are evenly distributed throughout the mixture.

4. Take teaspoons of the mixture and roll into balls about the size of a walnut. Space these out evenly on the prepared baking tray.

5. Use a fork to flatten each ball into a disc shape (you are not making fork biscuits as such: the biscuits will spread slightly during baking). Aim for each disc to measure roughly 4.5cm across. You may find it easier if your hands, and the fork, are slightly wet.

6. Bake for 7–8 minutes until they are just starting to go golden brown around the edges.

7. Leave to settle for a moment or two and then transfer to a wire cooling rack, using a small palette knife. They will still be soft at this stage but will firm up as they cool.

8. Once cool, store in an airtight container. Wrap them closely in foil inside the container to keep them extra fresh.

Picnic Biscuits

These scrumptious biscuits are practically a picnic in themselves. You can mix them by hand if you like, but it's easier in the food processor even though the mixture is quite stiff.

Makes about 28–30 biscuits

150g (5oz) butter, softened

110g (4oz) soft light brown sugar

150g (5oz) plain flour

2 level tsp baking powder

1 egg, beaten

50g (2oz) porridge oats

50g (2oz) desiccated coconut

75g (3oz) raisins and dried
  cranberries, mixed

You will need a large, greased
  baking tray.

1. Preheat the oven to 180°C (fan oven) or equivalent.

2. Whiz the softened butter and sugar together until soft and fluffy. Sieve in half of the flour and baking powder over the surface of the mixture and add the egg. Sieve in the rest of the flour and baking powder and whiz briefly.

3. Add the oats and coconut and whiz until thoroughly mixed. You may have to stop the machine a couple of times and scrape the mixture down from the sides with a flexible spatula. You may also want to stir the mixture slightly with a dinner knife as it is quite stiff.

4. Remove the blade from the machine and stir in the raisins and cranberries; a dinner knife works better than a spoon for this.

5. Take generous teaspoons of the mixture and roll into balls about the size of a walnut. Space these out evenly on the prepared baking tray. Use a fork to flatten each ball into a disc shape (you are not making fork biscuits as such: the biscuits will spread slightly during baking). It helps if the fork is wet, so have a jug of water handy.

6. You may need to bake the biscuits in two batches. Bake for 7–8 minutes until they are just starting to go golden brown around the edges.

7. Leave to settle for a moment or two and then transfer to a wire cooling rack, using a small palette knife. They will still be soft at this stage but will firm up as they cool.

8. Once cool, store in an airtight container: wrap them closely in foil inside the container to keep them extra fresh. The finished biscuits are more of a cookie than a crisp biscuit in consistency.

Totally Oaty Picnic Biscuits

These are very similar to the original Picnic Biscuits, but leave out the desiccated coconut and make up the quantity of oats to 110g (4oz).

Hiking Biscuits

Stir in 50g (2oz) dark chocolate chips along with the cranberries and raisins to either of the above recipes.

150g (5oz) butter, softened

110g (4oz) soft light brown sugar

150g (5oz) plain flour

2 level tsp baking powder

1 egg, beaten

50g (2oz) porridge oats

50g (2oz) desiccated coconut

75g (3oz) raisins and dried cranberries, mixed

You will need a large, greased baking tray.

1. Use a small palette knife to remove biscuits from baking trays. When your biscuits first come out of the oven they will be very soft and delicate. Leave them on the baking tray for a couple of minutes to firm up slightly. If you try to move them now they will crumble into pieces.

2. After a couple of minutes, they still won't be hard, but will be firm enough to move. If you leave them on the tray for too long, some biscuits can become stuck fast and you will have to practically chisel them off, breaking them in the process!

3. To remove the biscuits press as much of the blade of the palette knife as you can down flat against the surface of the baking tray, next to the biscuit. Use a sideways sweeping motion, and still keeping the blade pressed down, sweep it under the biscuit.

4. Transfer the biscuits to a cooling rack to cool and harden completely. As soon as they are cold, store them in an airtight container to keep them fresh – for extra insurance, wrap them closely in foil first.

Cheesy Biscuits

You can use plain or fancy cutters for these savoury biscuits: they are popular with all ages and equally at home at a drinks party or cut into simple novelty shapes for a children's tea party.

The smaller amount of cheese will make a slightly less rich biscuit, the greater amount will make a richer, cheesier one.

Makes about 15 depending on cutter size

50g (2oz) plain flour

Pinch of dry mustard powder

Pinch of salt

25g (1oz) butter, softened

75g–110g (3–4oz) well-flavoured
Cheddar cheese, grated

You will need a large greased
baking tray and some biscuit
cutters

1. Preheat the oven to 180°C (fan oven) or equivalent.

2. Tip the flour and mustard powder into the bowl of your food processor, sprinkle in the salt and add the butter.

3. Give the mixture a quick whizz to start everything off and add the cheese.

4. Keep whizzing, stopping from time to time to remove the lid and give the mixture a quick stir, until the mixture starts to clump together.

5. Stop the machine immediately and transfer the mixture to a clean board.

6. Gently bring the mixture together with your hands and knead it lightly until it looks and feels like a ball of cheesy marzipan.

7. Flour the board lightly and, using a floured rolling pin, roll out to a thickness of just less than 1cm.

8. Cut out your shapes and arrange on the prepared tray.

9. Reroll and cut out the rest.

10. Bake for 7–8 minutes, or until the biscuits are golden in colour.

11. Leave to settle on the tray for a few moments then remove carefully with a palette knife and finish cooling on a wire rack.

12. Once cold, store in an airtight container.

Malted Milk Biscuits

Children love making and eating these simple biscuits. They taste very like the malted milk biscuits you can buy in packets: the ones with the bobbly bits and pictures of cows stamped on them. You can cut them out in any shape you like but a cow shaped cutter would be perfect. Just a dessertspoonful of malt extract is all you need for a subtle, mild, child-friendly flavour and 50g of sugar is plenty, as the malt extract is naturally sweet. You can buy malt extract from Health Food shops.

Makes about 30, depending on cutter size

110g (4oz) softened butter

50g (2oz) caster sugar, ideally unrefined or golden

225g (8oz) plain flour

Tiny pinch of salt, optional

1 dessertspoon barley malt extract

4 dessertspoons semi-skimmed milk

You will need a large greased baking tray and a cutter, ideally cow shaped or rctangular

1. Preheat oven to 180°C (fan ovens) or equivalent.

2. Whiz the butter and sugar together until light and fluffy.

3. Add the flour and salt. Whiz to mix and add the malt extract and milk.

4. Whiz until the mixture starts to clump together, then stop the machine. You may have to do this in stages as the mixture is quite dense, removing the lid and scraping the mixture down from the sides three or four times, particularly at the beginning.

5. Scoop the mixture out of the machine and knead it lightly together on a floured board. Roll the dough to a thickness of just less than a pound coin.

6. Cut into shapes and transfer to the prepared baking sheet.

7. Bake for 6-8 minutes until the biscuits are pale golden and just tinged brown round the edges.

8. Leave to cool and harden for a couple of minutes, no more, on the tray, and then transfer to a cooling rack, using a palette knife.

9. Once they are completely cold, store in an airtight tin.

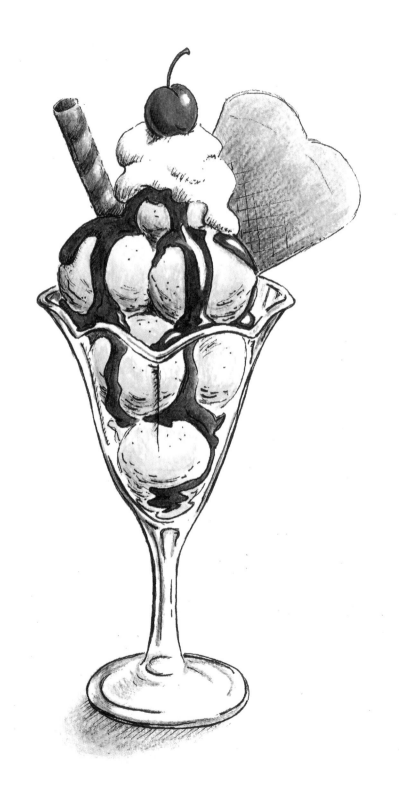

Chapter 10

Miscellaneous Recipes

Is there no end to the versatility of your food processor? You can whip up an unbelievably creamy ice cream from a simple frozen banana, or turn a few stale crusts into a crispy crumb coating. You can even make your own marzipan, which will taste far nicer than the commercial version and take you about five minutes to put together.

Marzipan

If you haven't tasted home-made marzipan before, you are in for a treat: it is quite different from the often over-sweet and cloying shop-bought versions. It's fresh and almondy and something that you want to eat in its own right, rather than as a bit of traditional decoration.

It's incredibly simple to make in your food processor: the only thing to watch out for is not to overprocess it: if you do, it will become oily and unmanageable.

110g (4oz) icing sugar

225g (8oz) ground almonds

1 very fresh egg yolk

½ tsp almond extract

3 tbsp lemon juice

1. Whizz the icing sugar in the processor to eliminate any clumps.

2. Add the ground almonds and whizz to blend them together.

3. Add the egg yolk, almond extract and lemon juice.

4. Whizz briefly to mix.

5. Stop and scrape the mixture down from the sides and whizz again.

6. The very second the mixture starts to congregate together on the side of the bowl stop immediately, otherwise the marzipan will become oily and overprocessed.

7. Take the mixture out of the processor, gathering up any loose crumbs, and form into a ball, working and kneading it gently with your hands.

8. The marzipan is now ready to use. If you are not using it straight away, wrap in cling film and keep cool and dry for up to 48 hours.

Covering a Cake with Home-made Marzipan

If you are using your **Marzipan** to cover a 23cm (9in) round Christmas or other celebration cake, here's how to do it.

1. Transfer the marzipan to a board lightly dusted with icing sugar.

2. Prepare your cake by brushing it with sieved apricot jam or marmalade.

3. Form the marzipan into a ball, rolling it between your hands for a few moments so that the warmth will make the marzipan more malleable.

4. Dust your rolling pin with icing sugar and carefully roll the marzipan flat – try to keep it circular in shape – until it is just a fraction bigger in circumference than the whole surface area of your cake including the top and sides.

5. Lift it carefully onto the glazed cake. You might find it easier to lift it by rolling it round your rolling pin and then unrolling it again over the cake.

6. Using both hands, gently and carefully smooth and shape the marzipan round the cake and trim the extra from around the bottom of the cake with a sharp knife.

7. Sieve a little more icing sugar over the top and smooth it gently with your rolling pin: if you happen to have a child's rolling pin it will make this bit easier!

8. Wrap the cake in clean greaseproof paper and keep in a cool dry place until ready to ice.

Magic Banana Ice Cream

You must try this simple ice cream that's incredibly easy to make: you won't believe how creamy the finished ice cream is, made from only one ingredient.

For best results the bananas should be perfectly ripe. It's fine if the skin is slightly speckled but the banana itself should still be creamy white. Don't attempt to freeze bananas with the skin on as it is a cold, thankless – and painful – task trying to peel a frozen banana.

1. Each banana should make enough ice cream for one person.

2. Peel the banana(s) and wrap them snugly in a freezer bag.

3. Put into the freezer and leave overnight or longer.

4. To make the ice cream, break the frozen banana(s) into several pieces.

5. Whizz in the food processor until smooth: your processor should be able to cope with two fairly large bananas at a time.

6. At first the banana will look stiff and crumbly, but have patience and keep going and you will soon have a smooth banana ice cream.

7. You may have to scrape the banana down from the sides of the food processor a couple of times with a flexible spatula or robust plastic picnic knife.

8. Eat immediately or put into a lidded freezer box and return to the freezer.

Breadcrumbs

It seems such a waste of money to buy packets of breadcrumbs while throwing away stale slices of bread, especially when it's so easy to make your own breadcrumbs in the processor.

All you need is a couple of slightly stale crusts or slices of bread: brown or white are both suitable.

Soft breadcrumbs and crisp breadcrumbs
There are two sorts of breadcrumbs: soft crumbs to use in bread sauce and some stuffings and puddings and treacle tarts, and crisp crumbs for coatings and toppings. Both are simple to make.

To make soft breadcrumbs
Tear the bread into rough pieces and put them into the processor bowl.
Whizz into crumbs.

To make crisp breadcrumbs
Tip the soft crumbs into a frying pan and dry fry with no oil at all over a moderate heat for a few minutes, stirring constantly with a wooden spoon.

Once the crumbs are crisp and toasty, leave them to cool. You may like to whizz them a second time for really fine crumbs.

You can store them, tightly sealed, in an airtight container for a few days. Alternatively, freeze until needed. Use straight from the freezer.

Tip
- Crispy crumbs add an extra dimension to baked pasta dishes and potato dishes. Scatter some on top, either on their own or mixed with grated cheese, before popping the dish into the oven.

Oven Toasted Chicken or Ham Sandwich

This makes a quick and tasty lunch or supper and proves just how easily leftovers can be transformed into a delicious treat with the help of your food processor. Serve with a green salad.

Per sandwich

Approximately 50g (2oz) cold cooked ham or cold cooked chicken – or a mixture of both

1 tsp mayonnaise

Freshly ground black pepper

2 slices of bread, buttered

1. Pre-heat your oven to 180C (fan oven) or equivalent

2. Using the cutting blade of your processor, lightly process the ham and or chicken very briefly until roughly minced.

3. Remove the processor blade and stir in the mayonnaise and season with black pepper.

4. Spread the filling over the buttered bread and sandwich in the usual way.

5. Cut the sandwich into 2 or 4 pieces and wrap in foil in a single layer.

6. Bake for about 10-15 minutes until the filling is piping hot and the bread is toasty.

7. Put it back into the oven with the foil open, for a further 3-5 minutes until the outside is crisp: you may like to turn the sandwich over after a couple of minutes to make sure both sides are of equal crispness.

Index